1,2 Samuel

Books in the Bible Study Commentary Series

Genesis — Leon J. Wood

Exodus — F. B. Huey, Jr.

Leviticus — Louis Goldberg

Numbers — F. B Huey, Jr.

Joshua — Paul P. Enns

Judges — Paul P. Enns

Ruth — Paul P. Enns

1, 2 Samuel — Howard F. Vos

Job — D. David Garland

Ecclesiastes — Louis Goldberg

Isaiah — D. David Garland

Jeremiah — F. B. Huey, Jr.

Daniel — Leon J. Wood

Hosea — D. David Garland

Amos — D. David Garland

Jonah — John H. Walton

Malachi — Charles D. Isbell

Matthew — Howard F. Vos

Mark — Howard F. Vos

Luke — Virtus E. Gideon

John — Herschel H. Hobbs

Acts — Curtis Vaughan

Romans — Curtis Vaughan and Bruce Corley

Galatians — Curtis Vaughan

Ephesians — Curtis Vaughan

Philippians — Howard F. Vos

Colossians and Philemon — Curtis Vaughan

The Thessalonian Epistles —John F. Walvoord

The Pastoral Epistles — E. M. Blaiklock

James — Curtis Vaughan

1, 2, 3 John — Curtis Vaughan

BIBLE STUDY COMMENTARY

1,2 Samuel

HOWARD F. VOS

ZONDERVAN
PUBLISHING HOUSE
OF THE ZONDERVAN CORPORATION
GRAND RAPIDS, MICHIGAN 49506

1, 2 SAMUEL: BIBLE STUDY COMMENTARY
Copyright © 1983 by The Zondervan Corporation
Grand Rapids, Michigan

Library of Congress Cataloging in Publication Data

Vos, Howard Frederic, 1925–
    1, 2 Samuel: Bible study commentary.

    Bibliography: p.
    1. Bible. O.T. Samuel—Commentaries. I. Title. II. Title: 1 and 2 Samuel. III. Title:
First and second Samuel.

BS1325.3.V67   1983   222'.407   83-1144
ISBN 0-310-33893-X

Edited by John Danilson

Printed in the United States of America

83 84 85 86 87 88 / 10 9 8 7 6 5 4 3 2 1

Contents

Introduction 7
1. The Judgeship of Samuel 13
2. The Rise of Saul 36
3. The Decline of Saul and the Rise of David (I) 59
4. The Decline of Saul and the Rise of David (II) 75
5. The Early Years of David's Reign 101
6. David's Conquests and His Sin 120
7. Absalom's Revolt and David's Restoration to Power 132
8. Concluding Aspects of David's Reign 152
   Bibliography 165

Introduction

The books of Samuel do not seem to strike the fancy of the Bible student to the degree that many other biblical books do. They provide no account of beginnings like Genesis, nor a prophecy of the end times like Revelation, nor a narrative of the life of Christ like the Gospels, nor an exalted statement of doctrine like Romans. Yet in their own way they are extremely important—historically, doctrinally, and devotionally. And they contain many stories familiar to the Sunday school student or even to society at large.

Historically, the books of Samuel provide links without which the Old Testament or the history of Israel would make no sense. They sketch the transition from the rule of the judges to kingship in Israel, portray the reign of Saul, and describe the exploits of David. They especially tell how David built the Hebrew empire and made Jerusalem its capital, giving it a significance it has to the present.

Doctrinally, these books have much to say about the nature of God: about His holiness, His preeminence over all the other gods, His demand to complete obedience on the part of His followers, and His judgment of sin. But they especially contribute the Davidic covenant (2 Sam. 7) which, along with the Abrahamic covenant (Gen. 12:1-3; 13:14-17; 15:4-21; 17:15-19), provides a basis for an ordering of the end times. Specifically God promised David a kingdom forever, a throne forever, and descendants to sit on that throne forever. Such grandiose promises could find satisfactory fulfillment only in David's greater Son, Jesus the Messiah, who will sit on the throne of David in the Holy City forever (cf. Ps. 2).

Devotionally, the books of Samuel provide endless lessons of spiritual and practical wisdom from the lives of such major figures as Samuel, Saul, and David, as well as numerous lesser-known Bible personalities. The biographical accounts one may read there are not just nice stories for entertainment; they depict actions and attitudes to be shunned or emulated.

The books of Samuel contain many stories that have an abiding interest. David's destruction of Goliath has become legendary. His adultery with Bathsheba is one of the best-known sins recorded in the Bible. His use of the lyre to quiet Saul's emotional upsets is a widely noted example of music therapy or of David's musicianship. Absalom's luxuriant hair and his abortive rebellion against David provide a familiar example of filial insubordination. The tender story of the infant Samuel, who was given to God by his parents and who at an early age heard the call of God for a life of devoted service, has been used to steer many a Sunday school child toward a life dedicated to God. And the account of the Philistine capture of the ark often has provided an example of the danger of trusting in the externalities of religion.

Name

These two books are named after Samuel, because he was the chief character in the first part and because he anointed Saul and David, the other two principal figures. During the days of the early church, the Hebrew Bible presented these two books as a unit. But Alexandrian Jews, who had produced the Greek translation (the Septuagint), linked Samuel with Kings and divided them both to produce four books of "The Kingdoms." The Latin translation (the Vulgate, completed about A.D. 400) altered the title to "Books of the Kings" and in time came to follow the Hebrew division between Samuel and Kings, speaking of 1 and 2 Samuel and 1 and 2 Kings. The Rabbinical Bible of Daniel Bomberg, published in Venice in 1517, adopted the Vulgate division and terminology; and that practice has been followed in the English versions and in the Western church generally.

Authorship and Date of Composition

Is is not known for certain who wrote the books of Samuel. Although a Jewish tradition names Samuel as author, this could not be more than partially true because his death is recorded in 1 Samuel 25:1 and 28:3. Though the death of David is not recorded, the reporting of his last words (2 Sam. 23:1–7) implies his demise. Moreover, on the basis of 1 Samuel 27:6, it is concluded that composition of the books did not come until after the division of the kingdom in 931 B.C. Reference there to possession of Ziklag by the kings of Judah "unto this day" apparently applies to a time after the kingdom of Judah had become a separate entity. Composition probably occurred, then, around 900 B.C. or a little later. The author presumably was a prophet in Judah, who certainly utilized accounts left by Samuel, Nathan, and Gad (1 Sam. 10:25; 1 Chron. 29:29), and perhaps others.

Contents and Outline

Primarily the purpose of the books of Samuel is to describe the founding of the Hebrew monarchy. Therefore they focus on the activities of Samuel as kingmaker, the career of Saul as only temporarily successful and ultimately a dismal failure, and the reign of David as the real founder of the Hebrew kingdom and of the dynasty out of which the Messiah would come. The books depict the establishment of Israel's religious and political center in Jerusalem and recount God's covenant with David, which forms the basis for the development of subsequent kingdom truth.

A secondary topic is the rise of the prophetic office in Israel. Samuel, the last of the judges, is mentioned in Acts 3:24 as the first of the prophets. He established schools of the prophets at Ramah (1 Sam. 19:20), Bethel (2 Kings 2:3), Jericho (2 Kings 2:5), and Gilgal (2 Kings 4:38).

The contents of Samuel may be outlined as follows:

I. The Judgeship of Samuel (1 Sam. 1:1–7:17)
   A. The Birth of Samuel and Hannah's Song (1:1–2:11)
      1. Hannah's grief (1:1–8)
      2. Hannah's prayer (1:9–18)
      3. Samuel's birth and dedication to God (1:19–28)
      4. Hannah's Song (2:1–10)
   B. The Childhood and Vision of Samuel (2:12–3:21)
      1. The failure of Eli's sons (2:12–17)
      2. Contrasting households (2:18–26)
      3. Announcement of judgment on Eli's house (2:27–36)
      4. The call of Samuel (3:1–21)
   C. Wars With the Philistines (4:1–7:17)
      1. Capture and return of the ark (4:1–7:2)
         a. Loss of the ark to the Philistines (4:1–11)
         b. Effect of the tidings at Shiloh (4:12–21)
         c. Devastation wrought by the ark (5:1–12)
         d. Return of the ark to Israel (6:1–7:2)
      2. Samuel's revival ministry and Philistine defeat (7:3–17)

II. The Rise of Saul (1 Sam. 8:1–15:35)
   A. Israel's Demand for a King (8:1–22)
   B. The Choice and Coronation of Saul (9:1–10:27)
   C. Saul's Accreditation by Victory (11:1–15)
   D. Samuel's Farewell Address (12:1–25)
   E. Victories Over the Philistines (13:1–14:52)
      1. Jonathan's surprise attack (14:1–15)
      2. Route of the Philistines (14:16–23)
      3. Saul's taboo and Jonathan's violation (14:24–35)

　　　　4. Jonathan's guilt and rescue (14:36–46)
　　　　5. General summary of Saul's family and his wars (14:47–52)
　　F. Saul's Disobedience and Rejection (15:1–35)

III. The Decline of Saul and the Rise of David (I) (16:1–20:42)
　　A. David's Anointing and Introduction to the Court (16:1–23)
　　B. David's Contest With Goliath (17:1–58)
　　C. David's Flight From Saul's Jealousy (18:1–20:42)
　　　　1. David's acceptance by the royal family (18:1–5)
　　　　2. David's popularity and Saul's jealousy (18:6–30)
　　　　3. Jonathan as mediator (19:1–7)
　　　　4. Two more attempts on David's life (19:8–17)
　　　　5. David's flight to Ramah (19:18–23)
　　　　6. David's parting from Jonathan (20:1–42)

IV. The Decline of Saul and the Rise of David (II) (21:1–30:31)
　　A. David's Wanderings (21:1–30:31)
　　　　1. David at Nob (21:1–9)
　　　　2. David at Gath (21:10–15)
　　　　3. Wanderings in Judah and Moab (22:1–5)
　　　　4. Saul's war council and the Nob massacre (22:6–23)
　　　　5. Rescue of Keilah (23:1–13)
　　　　6. Wandering in the wilderness of Ziph (23:14–28)
　　　　7. David in the wilderness of En Gedi (23:29–24:22)
　　　　8. David, Nabal, and Abigail (25:1–44)
　　　　9. David's second sparing of Saul (26:1–25)
　　　　10. David among the Philistines (27:1–12)
　　　　11. Saul's fate pronounced (28:1–25)
　　　　12. David's dismissal from the Philistine army (29:1–11)
　　　　13. Tragedy at Ziklag and Amalekite defeat (30:1–31)
　　B. Saul's Death (31:1–13)

V. The Early Years of David's Reign (2 Sam. 1:1–7:29)
　　A. David as King at Hebron (1:1–5:5)
　　　　1. News of Saul's death (1:1–16)
　　　　2. David's lament (1:17–27)
　　　　3. David's move to Hebron (2:1–7)
　　　　4. Rivalry with the kingdom of Israel (2:8–3:1)
　　　　5. Rise of David and decline of the house of Saul (3:2–39)
　　　　　　a. Growth of the house of David (3:2–5)
　　　　　　b. Abner's disaffection and assassination (3:6–39)
　　　　6. Murder of Ish-Bosheth and punishment of his murderers
　　　　　　(4:1–12)
　　　　7. David's acceptance by all the tribes (5:1–5)

B. David's Consolidation of the Kingdom (5:6–6:23)
   1. David at Jerusalem (5:6–16)
   2. David's victories over the Philistines (5:17–25)
   3. Bringing the ark to Jerusalem (6:1–23)
C. The Davidic Covenant (7:1–29)

VI. David's Conquests and His Sin (2 Sam. 8:1–12:31)
   A. Summary of Conquests (8:1–14)
   B. Administrative Details (8:15–9:13)
   C. The Ammonite War (10:1–11:1; 12:26–31)
   D. David's Sin (11:2–27)
   E. Judgment on David and His Repentance (12:1–25)

VII. Absalom's Revolt and David's Restoration to Power
    (2 Sam. 13:1–20:26)
   A. Amnon's Incest and Absalom's Revenge (13:1–39)
   B. Absalom's Return to Jerusalem (14:1–33)
   C. Absalom's Revolt (15:1–12)
   D. David's Flight (15:13–16:14)
   E. Absalom in Jerusalem (16:15–17:23)
   F. Defeat and Death of Absalom (17:24–18:18)
   G. David's Mourning for Absalom (18:19–19:8)
   H. David's Restoration to Power (19:9–20:26)

VIII. Concluding Aspects of David's Reign (2 Sam. 21:1–24:25)
   A. The Famine (21:1–14)
   B. Exploits of David's Warriors (21:15–22)
   C. David's Song (22:1–51)
   D. The Last Words of David (23:1–7)
   E. Catalog of David's Mighty Men (23:8–39)
   F. Census and Plague (24:1–25)

For Further Study

1. In Bible dictionaries or encyclopedias or books on the Old Testament, read further on the authorship of the books of Samuel.

2. Try to read through 1 Samuel in one sitting; this will take about one and a half hours. While doing so ask the following questions.
   a. What events stand out in my mind and why?
   b. What doctrinal concepts impress themselves on my mind?
   c. What devotional thoughts make an impact on my heart and life?

3. Try to read through 2 Samuel in one sitting, a task requiring about an hour. While doing so ask the questions suggested in No. 2 above.

Chapter 1

The Judgeship of Samuel
(1 Samuel 1:1–7:17)

The sacred historian drew aside the curtain of time to reveal a dramatic chain of events that was destined to transform the Hebrews from a loose collection of Semitic tribes into a powerful nation. As he began his narrative in 1 Samuel, Israel was weak, disunited, and powerless before the warlike Philistines. By the time he concluded his account in 2 Samuel, the kingdom had been established under the reign of Saul; and David had subdued the Philistines and other enemies of Israel and had established a vigorous kingdom respected throughout the Near East.

The sacred scribe began his story with events early in the eleventh century B.C. when the aged Eli was the high priest and judge of Israel. Spiritual conditions in the land were at a low ebb, and the Philistines threatened the very existence of the Hebrews. Since Eli evidently was incapable of controlling either his wicked sons or the wayward populace and was getting on in years, God needed to find another leader to shepherd His people. Therefore 1 Samuel begins with the provision of Samuel, who was to become the new leader.

A. The Birth of Samuel and Hannah's Song (1:1–2:11)

1. *Hannah's grief* (1:1–8)

The new leader was a long time in coming. In fact, his mother almost despaired of having any children. The first verses of 1 Samuel describe circumstances leading up to Samuel's birth. The town from which Samuel's family came was Ramathaim (v. 1), or Ramah (v. 19), a place of uncertain identification in the hill country of Ephraim in central Palestine. Some would locate it at modern Rentis, about eighteen miles west of Shiloh and eight miles northeast of Lydda (also called Lod). Samuel's father was Elkanah, a Zuphite (the region of Zuph also cannot be positively located) of Levitical descent. His genealogy is given more at length in 1 Chronicles 6:22–23, 33–34.

In contrast to the prevailing lack of religious interest among the Hebrews, Elkanah and his family were simple, pious people who faithfully worshiped Yahweh. But even in his piety Elkanah practiced polygamy. His home life reminds us of the fact that during the period of the judges, "everyone did as he saw fit" (Judg. 21:25 NIV). In this case Elkanah may have taken a second wife, Peninnah, because his first wife, Hannah, had no children, and he wanted a son to keep his name alive. How many children Peninnah had is not specified, but there must have been at least four. Verse 4 mentions sons and daughters; so there must have been at least two of each.

Obedient to the instructions of the law, Elkanah went "year by year"[1] to sacrifice at Shiloh (v. 3). The occasion presumably was the Passover, which Hebrews were required to observe (Exod. 13:10). There is no intimation here of obedience to the injunction that required males to present themselves at the sanctuary three times a year (Deut. 16:16). Shiloh is to be identified with the mound of Seilun, about twenty miles north of Jerusalem, and there the tabernacle was set up when the Israelites entered Canaan (Josh. 18:1). The object of Elkanah's adoration was "Yahweh of Hosts" (v. 3), which may refer to God as Ruler over the sun, moon, and stars, or over the heavenly beings who bow before Him, or as the Leader of His people in battle. In any case He was revered as the majestic, sovereign, omnipotent Lord.

In marked contrast to the piety and sacrifice of Elkanah is the impiety and rapaciousness of Eli's two sons, Hophni and Phinehas. They appear here without comment but later are subjected to divine condemnation. The opening chapters of the Samuel narrative is interspersed with the record of judgment on the family of Eli. When the account focuses on Samuel, there are allusions to Eli's sons. When Eli's wicked family is at center stage, pious Samuel is in the wings. The sacred historian moves skillfully between the two spiritual opposites.

But the mention of Hophni and Phinehas involved more than a literary device; they were officiating priests at the sacrifices. After a person made a peace offering, he received back a good part of the sacrificial animal to be eaten by himself and his family in a social feast before God. On those occasions Elkanah gave adequate helpings to Peninnah and her children; but to Hannah he gave "one portion for two persons" (v. 5; "a double portion," NIV). This was an Oriental practice of showing special regard for a beloved or distinguished guest (cf. Gen. 43:34). By it Elkanah sought to express his love for Hannah in as great a way as he would have if she had borne him a child. Elkanah's greater love for Hannah led her rival, Peninnah, to "taunt her to annoy her" (v. 6 JB), or "provoke her to irritate her"—to create in her great consternation or agony, not exactly to make her angry. Hannah's customary response was to become so morose that

---

[1]When the version from which biblical phrases have come is not specified, the translations appearing in this commentary are the author's own. Unless otherwise indicated, proper names are generally according to the New International Version.

she could not eat. Elkanah would try to comfort her by declaring that he was better to her than a large family would have been.

2. *Hannah's prayer* (1:9–18)

Hannah's grief finally became too great for her to bear. On one occasion after a sacrificial meal at Shiloh, she poured out her soul in great anguish to God in the "temple" (v. 7; literally, the "palace" of Yahweh). This was so-called because it was the dwelling place of Yahweh of Hosts, not because it was a magnificent building. Seated at the doorway, Eli could observe the movements of worshipers; and he watched Hannah. She was weeping bitterly and actually was engaged in extended prayer. Only the vow from that prayer is recorded here. It contained two points. If God would give her a son, she would (1) dedicate him to the Lord for lifelong service and (2) set him apart as a Nazirite for his entire life. Scripture did not require either of these commitments to be lifelong. A Nazirite was a person especially separated or dedicated to God. Regulations concerning such a vow appear in Numbers 6:1–8, 13–21. Samson and John the Baptist were, like Samuel, lifelong Nazirites.

Perhaps it is valid to speculate that if God had answered Hannah's prayer for a son earlier in life, she might have kept him for herself. In her extremity she came to the point that she was willing to commit him totally to God. God wanted an especially prepared mother to give birth to this key figure in the history of Israel—one who would hold together the nation for an extended period and then would inaugurate the monarchy and anoint the first two kings of Israel. Hannah was only one of several women whom God especially prepared to give birth to key figures in redemption history (others would include Sarah, mother of Isaac; Elizabeth, mother of John the Baptist; and the Virgin Mary, mother of Jesus).

Hannah's silent utterance was uncommon in early Hebrew prayer; and finally Eli thought her to be drunk, an intimation that there was a considerable amount of drinking during sacrificial meals at the sanctuary. She declared, "I am a sober person" (v. 15 NEB) and insisted that she was not a "daughter of Belial" (v. 16 KJV; "base woman," RSV). After she explained her great vexation of spirit while petitioning God, the kindly old priest replied, "May the God of Israel grant your request." This expression is not to be considered as a prediction or promise but a pious wish. Encouraged by Eli's word, Hannah went away believing her prayer would be answered. No longer downcast, she presumably returned to her interrupted sacrificial meal and ate.

3. *Samuel's birth and dedication to God* (1:19–28)

As was customary in a land where it gets light very early, Elkanah's family arose early the next morning to make good use of the daylight hours for travel. Before departure, they "worshiped" (v. 19; literally, "prostrated themselves") before God. The great reverence for God expressed by both Old and New Testament believers should prove instructive to contemporary religionists for whom God often is "the Good Buddy upstairs." To be sure, God wants to be a Friend of sinners and wants them to be His friends as well; but He is after all, the holy, sovereign Master of the universe and those in it. The proper response that such majesty deserves is expressed in Isaiah 6:1-8. After Elkanah and his family returned home, in due time God "remembered" (v. 19) Hannah, i.e., He acted in kindness toward her and answered her prayer.

"In due time" (v. 20), or perhaps better "at the end of a year," and thus about time for the family's annual pilgrimage, Hannah gave birth to a son. She called him Samuel, the meaning of which may be "heard of God" or "name of God." In either case Hannah's statement, "Because I asked the LORD for him" (v. 20), is an expression based on the facts, not an explanation of the meaning of the name.

Shortly after Samuel's birth, it was time for the annual sacrifice at Shiloh. Hannah expressed the desire to absent herself from the sanctuary until her son was weaned (at three years of age). Then it was her plan to present Samuel at the tabernacle and leave him there the rest of his life. Elkanah consented to Hannah's wish and added, "May the LORD establish His word" (v. 23), i.e., fulfill it. Since there is no indication in this passage that God had delivered a special revelation concerning the birth of Samuel, Elkanah probably had in mind Eli's pronouncement in verse 17. The father possibly had some further hope that God would prosper the child by giving him life and health so he could be left at the sanctuary some day. In a society with a relatively high infant mortality rate, Elkanah's expression was no idle wish. The Jerusalem Bible translates, "May Yahweh bring about what you have said" (v. 23).

Then Elkanah went to Shiloh with the rest of the family "to offer the annual sacrifice" and "to fulfil his vow" (v. 21). Some conclude that since there is no previous record of Elkanah's vow, this reference must be an insertion of a scribe. Others suggest that Elkanah had joined Hannah in making a vow to God or that he had made her vow his own. Yet others would follow the Septuagint, which says he fulfilled his "vows" and paid his "tithes" on this occasion (cf. Num. 18:26-29; Elkanah was a Levite). The latter suggestion seems more plausible because Elkanah's going to Shiloh and making a sacrifice would not have fulfilled any vow to present Samuel, who was still at home.

When Hannah weaned her son, she fulfilled her vow and brought him to Shiloh. Also, she brought a handsome offering consisting of an ephah (about a half bushel) of flour, a skin of wine (probably a goatskin), and a three-year-old bull (v. 24). The traditional Hebrew text (the basis for the KJV) has "three bulls," but the Septuagint and the Dead Sea Scrolls give "a three-year-old bull," the commonly accepted reading in the newer versions. After the sacrifice of the bull and the inevitable fellowship or sacramental meal that followed, Elkanah and Hannah brought Samuel to Eli.

Naturally Hannah took the lead in explaining what was about to happen, for she had made the fervent prayer for a child in Eli's presence some four years before. Reminding the priest of her prayer on that earlier occasion, she proceeded to divulge the content of her prayer and the vow she had made. God had granted her request and had given her the son for whom she had pleaded. Now she was fulfilling her vow and "giving" (v. 28; not "lending" as in the KJV) her son to God all the rest of his life. Evidently Elkanah concurred with Hannah or else she never could have given away a son in that patriarchal society. Concurrence is underscored in the rendering of verse 28, with some ancient manuscripts and several ancient translations reading, "And *they* worshiped the LORD there." However, it is not necessary to abandon the traditional reading "and he worshiped." In the latter case the inference would be that Elkanah worshiped, and Hannah followed with her beautiful song in 2:1–10. Reference hardly could be to the worship of Samuel, who was only three years old. After the presentation the account records simply that Elkanah and his family returned to Ramah and left Samuel behind (2:11). That Samuel need not have been a burden to Eli is evident from the fact that women ministering at the sanctuary were available to care for him (cf. 2:22).

The action of Hannah and Elkanah in giving their son to God for His purposes is a tremendous example to modern believing parents. Often they stand in the way of their offsprings' desire to serve God, selfishly blocking their efforts to go to a foreign mission field or to engage in some seemingly "insignificant" task that does not appear prestigious enough or lucrative enough to bring credit to the family.

How Scripture glosses over, or totally ignores, the pathos or trauma of the dramas it depicts! Here there is nothing of the heart-wrenching parting of Hannah from the son for whom she had agonized for so long. There is nothing of the sobs of the young child as his mother left him with total strangers. There is nothing in the subsequent narrative of the lonely hours that both mother and son must have suffered during months and years to come. Perhaps God gave supernatural comfort to both as He has done so often in other cases where service to God has required parting and loneliness.

4. *Hannah's Song* (2:1–10)

Whatever distress of spirit Hannah may have experienced over parting with Samuel, it did not surface in her magnificent song, which ranks as one of the greatest in the Bible. Though it expressed her triumph and thanksgiving, the song was not narrowly personal but recognized in Hannah's own experience the workings of a holy God in the midst of His people. And her paean of praise exuded a confidence for the future that involved a prediction of the coming of Messiah.

Often critics suggest that the author or redactor of Samuel put this psalm into the mouth of Hannah. They say it was composed by an unknown person, or by David, at a later time. But it seems inconceivable that a psalm of David should be attributed to an unknown like Hannah. Presumably the sacred historian found it ascribed to Hannah in the sources he used. To assert that a simple person like Hannah was incapable of such elevated phraseology is to deny the prophetic inspiration of the pious by the Holy Spirit. Such a denial raises questions about the ability of the Virgin Mary to utter the Magnificat (Luke 1:46–55) or of a simple fisherman like John to write the tremendous passages attributed to him. Moreover, refusal to accept Hannah's authorship of this poem tends to be accompanied by a misconstruing of its meaning or significance and an attempt to turn it into a song of victory in battle.

The song begins with a doxology (2:1–2). Hannah's joy is solely in God. In her moment of ecstasy she likens herself to an animal (perhaps an ox) with horns (a symbol of strength) lifted high in the air. But she is careful to specify that her strength is "in the LORD" (2:1). Her mouth, formerly closed in the presence of her enemy, now is open to praise God because His might has brought "deliverance" (NIV). God the Holy One is the Rock, the One on whom a person can rest his or her confidence (2:2; cf. Ps. 91:1–2). For the righteous this Rock provides a perfect place of refuge, but the wicked cannot stand before divine holiness. They are dashed by the Rock.

The song proceeds with a warning to God's opponents (2:3–8). The Holy One of Israel, the One in whom the righteous can always trust, effectively governs all people. The proud, self-sufficient opponents of God are warned to keep silent, not to vent their insolent or arrogant words against the righteous. The holy Governor is omniscient. He "knows" all things, and "with him deeds are weighed" (2:3). This latter clause may be interpreted to mean that God properly "estimates" the deeds of the wicked and finds them not to be firmly founded or established. Or, more probably, it may mean that the acts of God are weighed and found to be just or righteous. Those righteous acts are then described in His comparative handling of the righteous and the wicked (vv. 4–8). This interpretation seems to lie behind the NEB translation "he governs all that men do" in verse 3.

The contrast between the lot of the wicked and the righteous under the governing hand of God comes clear in 2:4–8. "The bows of the warriors are broken" (NIV) or "Strong men stand in mute dismay" (NEB), while "those who faltered put on new strength" (NEB). The rich who had plenty will find it necessary to hire themselves out for bread, but the poor who were hungry hunger no more. The mother of many children pines away because she has lost all her sons, but the barren woman has seven children—the full number of divine blessing. Verse 6 should be viewed figuratively and probably means that one is brought to the lowest state of degradation, to the very point of death, but is spared or rescued and restored to happiness.

In 2:7 the contrast is switched to poverty and riches, to humiliation and exaltation: "The LORD sends poverty and wealth; he humbles and he exalts" (NIV). Verse 8 describes God's care of the poor and weak. "Dust" and the "ash heap" connote deepest degradation; the town dump ("ash heap") was the place where beggars slept at night. The righteous judge, who extends favor to the helpless, raises such beggars to enjoy seats of honor. To Hannah, this exaltation marked the comparative change in her social position as a result of the birth of her son. Verse 8 goes on to say that Yahweh exercises this governance as the One who has created and now sustains the whole created order.

The song concludes with a statement of the believer's confidence (2:9–10). "The footsteps of his saints [or 'loyal ones'] he will keep" so they do not stumble and fall into adversity. But the wicked, who turn away from divine light and who oppress the righteous, will "perish in darkness," or fall into calamity, for one does not become strong by mere "brute strength" but by the Spirit of God (Zech. 4:6). "As for Yahweh, those who contend against [stand against as in a court action] him are shattered." Against such He will "thunder," demonstrate His omnipotent might, in a display of judgment to the very "ends of the earth." As God will throw down His foes in judgment, He will "give strength to his king," the One who will uphold His justice and right. He will "raise high the head ['horn'] of his anointed." Reference here is first to the kingship soon to be established in Israel; but the ultimate reference has to be to the ideal King, or Messiah (anointed One), who would one day rise in that kingly line and who would make all His enemies His footstool (Matt. 22:44; Acts 2:35). Ultimate victory, or victory in the long run, provides confidence for the believer in the short run. God's ultimate victory cannot be assured unless He has superintending power along the way.

B. The Childhood and Vision of Samuel (2:12–3:21)

1. *The failure of Eli's sons* (2:12–17)

In contrast to the piety of Hannah and Elkanah and trusting little Samuel, Eli's sons were "scoundrels" (2:12) or "sons of Belial," (Heb.) and "had no regard for the LORD," or "did not know" (NASB) Him. They did not know Him as they should have known Him. That is, they did not truly reverence Him or trouble themselves about the requirements of divine service and the proper conduct of servants of God.

The arrangement prescribed in the law of Moses for thank offerings, with which a fellowship meal was associated, was as follows. First the fat portions were burned on the altar as a sacrifice to God. Then the breast and right thigh, dedicated to God, were given to the priest for his support. The rest of the animal could be cooked and eaten by an offerer and his family (cf. Lev. 7:30–34). Eli's sons violated that arrangement in two ways. First, they took far more than was due them by having a servant dip into the family's kettle with a three-pronged fork and take out all the fork would hold. Moreover, even before the cooking began, they sometimes sent a servant around to demand choice cuts of meat. Thus they deprived the offerer of what was rightfully his. Second, they frequently demanded their share even before God was properly honored with the burnt offering.

God viewed this sin of Eli's sons as very grave because they "treated Yahweh's offering with contempt" (2:17). They insulted God by not worshiping properly, and their disregard for God and His prescribed order of worship inevitably would rub off on the laity. The NEB translation points up this result: "they brought the LORD's sacrifice into general contempt." And if the sanctuary at Shiloh became so corrupted that it no longer fulfilled its purpose, then God Himself might be forced to bring judgment on it and destroy it utterly.

2. Contrasting households (2:18–26)

In these verses the piety of Samuel and his mother and father are sharply contrasted with the wickedness of Eli's sons. "Samuel continued serving Yahweh, a boy girded with a linen ephod" (2:18). Samuel served God at the sanctuary, no doubt doing what the venerable Eli instructed him to do, and ministering devotedly alongside Eli's "scoundrel" sons. The ephod was a sleeveless apron-like garment worn by priests, Levites, and eminent persons (e.g., David, 2 Sam. 6:14) at religious festivals. Samuel wore a garment like this even as a boy because he had been dedicated to God for lifelong service. As he grew, year by year his mother brought him a "coat" (KJV), or "robe," a sleeveless outer garment with a hole for the head and slits in the sides for the arms to come through. This woolen robe, which reached almost to the ground, was worn by prophets (1 Sam. 15:27), kings (1 Chron. 15:27), and women of rank (2 Sam. 13:18).

Eli "would bless Elkanah and his wife" periodically as they came to see Samuel and bring him the robe. The blessing evidently was not merely a pious wish but an efficacious prophetic utterance. And God rewarded this pious couple for their devotion by giving them three sons and two daughters. Meanwhile, Samuel "grew up in the presence of Yahweh"— under His protection the blessing at the sanctuary. "Grew" may involve moral and intellectual as well as physical growth (cf. Exod. 2:10–11).

In contrast to the spiritual perception and dedication of Samuel and his family is now juxtaposed once more the degradation of Eli's sons. Not only did they ignore the divinely imposed sacrificial regulations, but they also violated the women who served at the tabernacle. It is not necessary to conclude that Hophni and Phinehas had introduced the ritual prostitution of Canaanite worship at the sanctuary, as some commentators suggest. It seems rather that they simply committed fornication with the women who had devoted themselves to the service of God at the tabernacle. When reports of the conduct of his sons came to Eli, he admonished them. He pointed out, first, that the effect of their action was devastating. They were "causing Yahweh's people to sin" (2:24). Second, he observed that when one person sins against another, God could serve as Mediator. But if one sins against God, there is no one to intercede.

Eli's sons refused to pay any attention to their aged father, "for Yahweh was resolved to slay them" (2:25). Bible students often stumble over such statements, concluding that God sometimes hardens human hearts just so He can punish them. Admittedly we shall never understand fully how sovereignty and free will work together, but Scripture clearly indicates that God "delights in mercy" (Mic. 7:18) and invites all who so desire to come to Him (Rev. 22:17). When people disregard the truth of God long enough, however, God may give them up (Rom. 1:24, 26–28) and may even bring some judicial hardening of their hearts. It should be noted that Pharaoh of Egypt hardened his own heart several times before God is said to have hardened it once (Exod. 9:12). And the Pharisees had enjoyed numerous gracious opportunities to receive the Messiah; but their opposition became so determined that Jesus finally pronounced their case hopeless and gave them no further opportunity to believe. After Eli's sons had opposed God's ways long enough, He "resolved to slay them" (2:25).

The passage closes by introducing Samuel once more in marked contrast with Eli's sons. Samuel "was growing in stature and in favor with God and with men" (2:26). A higher commendation could hardly be given, for the statement is almost identical to the words describing the development of the child Jesus as He grew up in Nazareth almost eleven hundred years later and about forty miles to the north (Luke 2:52).

3. Announcement of judgment on Eli's house (2:27–36)

Before God caused His wrath to fall on Eli's wicked house, He sent a "man of God," an unnamed prophet, to announce the coming judgment (2:27). The prophet rehearsed the grace that Eli and his house had received from Yahweh and the ingratitude and wickedness of his sons. Then he predicted judgment on Eli's house with the consequent impoverishment of his descendants.

The prophet observed that God had chosen Eli's ancestor in Egypt to keep His sanctuary. This reference evidently was to Aaron. Though the

Old Testament does not reveal the genealogy of Eli, it is clear that he was descended from Ithamar, fourth son of Aaron (1 Chron. 24:3). Not only had God bestowed high honor on the house of Aaron, He also had provided adequate remuneration in the offerings of the Israelites.

Then, speaking for God, the man of God leveled this charge against Eli: "Why do you kick at" (NASB), or "tread with your feet," or "show disrespect for my sacrifice" (2:29)? Eli was linked with the conduct of his sons. And by tolerating the abuses of his sons, he was adjudged guilty of honoring his sons more than God. The fattening of themselves with the "choicest of every sacrificial gift of Israel" (v. 29) was a sin already described in verses 15–17. For bringing the worship of God into disrepute they would suffer greatly. To be sure, God had promised that "your house" (Eli's family) and "your father's house" (Eli's relatives in other lines descended from Aaron) would indeed "walk before me forever" (2:30). That is, they would continue to serve as priests at the sanctuary and thus walk before God (cf. Exod. 29:9, "a perpetual statute" with Aaron and his sons). While God had no intention of revoking that commitment ("Be it far from me" 2:30 KJV), He would not permit a false trust in that pledge to let a dishonoring of the priestly office go unpunished. He would "cut off the arm" (2:31), i.e., destroy the strength or vital energy of Eli's house and cause his descendants to die young. For fulfillment see, for example, 1 Samuel 4:11; 22:18–23; 1 Kings 2:27.

Although God would confer numerous benefits on His people, "oppression" (2:32; "distress,") would befall His "dwelling." Fulfillment of this calamitous prediction began at the end of Eli's life when the Philistines captured the ark (1 Sam. 4:11). When the ark was returned, it was not restored to the tabernacle but remained at Kiriath Jearim for a number of years. Subsequently, the tabernacle itself was removed to Nob, where a massacre of priests occurred (1 Sam. 21:1–2). Later yet it was moved to Gibeon (1 Chron. 16:39; 21:29). With all of these developments the sanctuary lost much of its prestige. Verse 33 makes it clear that God had no intention of going back on His word to the house of Aaron and Eli; but their descendants who served at the tabernacle would pine away with grief over the decay of the national shrine, and they would die in the prime of life. As a sign of Eli that He meant what He said, God then announced the death of his sons, Hophni and Phinehas, on the same day.

In their place God determined to raise up a "faithful priest," who would obey His will (2:35). The primary reference was to Samuel but the secondary and fuller reference must be to Zadok, whom Solomon made priest in place of Abiathar (Eli's great-grandson). That action is stated to be the fulfillment of the prophecy (1 Kings 2:27). Zadok's descendants did indeed walk before God's "anointed" (1 Sam. 2:35), the kings of Israel. The term "always" means these priest maintained themselves in the sanctuary at Jerusalem until the destruction of the temple by the Babylonians in 586 B.C. Moreover, the sons of Zadok will perform God's service in the future kingdom of God on earth in the millennial temple, according to the vision of Ezekiel (Ezek. 40:46; 43:19; 44:15; 48:11). Thus the "anointed," before whom the "faithful priest" would walk "always," was not merely the king—Solomon, David, and his descendants—but the Son of David, whose kingdom will be everlasting.

Deprived of the high priesthood and no longer enjoying the abundance of Hophni and Phinehas, the posterity of Eli in their poverty would have to bow down to the high priest to secure some menial task so they could earn a "piece of silver" or "loaf of bread" (2:36). But Samuel's descendants also continued to minister before the king. His grandson Heman, "the king's seer," was placed by David over the choir in the house of God (1 Chron. 6:33; 25:4–5).

4. *The call of Samuel* (3:1–21)

Having narrated the divine judgment on Eli and his house, the sacred historian now proceeds to describe God's call of the "faithful priest" who would lead Israel in the following decades. While Samuel was growing up and serving the Lord before Eli, the word of Yahweh was "rare" (3:1), or "seldom heard." That is, revelation of the will and purpose of Yahweh as received in prophetic vision was extremely infrequent, presumably both because of the corruption of the priesthood and the waywardness of the populace. In that time of spiritual barrenness, God called Samuel. Following Josephus, many commentators have concluded that Samuel was twelve at the time. But, or course, there is no way of knowing his exact age.

The young Samuel was sleeping in the tabernacle, probably in a cell in the court, but possibly in the holy place near the sevenbranched lampstand. That piece of furniture had little cups at the end of each of its arms. Fresh olive oil was poured into the cups each morning and the lamps were rekindled. Since the lamps had not yet gone out, the time of the call must have been early morning. Because Eli was nearly blind and often needed assistance and because Samuel had never before received any divine communication, the lad assumed when he heard a voice that Eli was calling for help. Samuel responded three times to what he believed to be Eli's voice. Each time the aged priest sent him back to his bedroll. Finally Eli surmised that God was calling the youngster and instructed him accordingly.

"Yahweh . . . came and stood" (3:10) in an objectively real sense. Samuel had a vivid sense of God's presence, for this was no mere dream. When Samuel responded as Eli had told him to, God addressed him with articulate words in a physically audible voice. The contents of the message could leave Samuel in no doubt as to the identity of the Speaker. God announced that He would not only execute judgment on the house of Eli but also would bring about disasters that would cause ears to "tingle" (3:11 or "ring") with astonishment and horror (cf. 2 Kings 21:12; Jer. 19:3). "From beginning to end" (3:12) indicates the thoroughness of the execution of judgment. "I have sworn" (v. 14) demonstrates that the sentence was irrevocable.

Then "Samuel lay down until morning" (3:15). The text does not say he slept. What one of us could have slept after a meeting with the sovereign God of the universe and after having heard a pronouncement of judgment on our benefactor and guardian, together with an intimation of some larger woe to fall on the whole community? There is no hint of what went through Samuel's mind during the following hours. But at length it was time for Samuel to get up and busy himself with the early morning tasks, such as opening the doors of the sanctuary. Though the biblical narrative nowhere details the construction of a more permanent "temple" after the Hebrews had entered Canaan, evidently that had taken place; the desert tabernacle with its curtains probably had disintegrated during the centuries since its construction.

Naturally Samuel was afraid to tell Eli what God had said, but the old priest demanded an accounting. "May God do so to you, and more also" (3:17) was a form of a curse originally connected with the slaying of an animal at the taking of an oath. The parties pledged or petitioned that the fate of the victim would befall them if they broke the oath. Then Samuel told Eli "everything" (v. 18). Eli's response was eloquent in its simplicity: "It is the LORD." The statement indicated (1) his devotion to God; (2) his quiet resignation to the judgment of God that he knew to be right; and (3) his recognition of the fact that God had indeed spoken to Samuel. Samuel's action in making a full revelation to his mentor and guardian took great courage and gave some indication that he had the fortitude to be God's prophet to the people of Israel.

The spotlight next focuses on Samuel and his ministry. He "grew" —physically, mentally, and spiritually; "the LORD was with him" (3:19)—His presence assured the validity of his prophetic message; and "let none of his words fall to the ground"—left no word unfulfilled that He spoke through Samuel. So all Israel, from Dan at the northern border to Beersheba at the southern border (a distance of about one hundred fifty miles), knew that Samuel was an accredited prophet of Yahweh. Even though Samuel's activity centered in the vicinity of Ramah, evidently his counsel was sought by individuals throughout Israel. Thus his spiritual authority was widely recognized. And "Yahweh continued to appear" (3:21) to Samuel at Shiloh, revealing Himself to the prophet for his edification and instructing him in regard to his leadership of Israel.

C. Wars With the Philistines (4:1–7:17)

1. *Capture and return of the ark* (4:1–7:2)

a) *Loss of the ark to the Philistines* (4:1–11)

While Samuel was maturing and winning the respect of Israel, and while God was preparing to execute judgment on the house of Eli, the Philistines continued to encroach on Hebrew territory. Expanding from their base along the Mediterranean in southwestern Palestine, the Philistines gradually moved up the valleys into the highlands. The Hebrews decided to challenge the Philistines near Aphek, a strategically located site at the headwaters of the Yarkon River, about ten miles northeast of modern Tel Aviv. While the Philistines camped at Aphek, the Hebrews camped at Ebenezer, now identified with Izbet Sartah, about two miles east of Aphek. The initial encounter was costly for the Hebrews; they suffered almost four thousand casualties, who perhaps were mowed down by Philistine chariotry. On the face of it there is no reason why the Hebrews should have won. The Philistines held superiority in metallurgy and their effort to deprive the Hebrews of iron (1 Sam. 13:19) gave them an overwhelming military advantage. But the Hebrews were accustomed to having God fight battles for them; and when they lost on this occasion, they anguished, "Why did God defeat us?" (4:3).

Apparently they failed to keep in mind that God will not bless people who turn from Him and enter into idolatrous practices (1 Sam. 7:3). Probably they would not have appealed to aged Eli, then ninety-eight (1 Sam. 4:15), to intercede with God on their behalf, for he was no longer able to be very active in the work of God. And certainly the conduct of Hophni and Phinehas would not have inspired them to self-searching or a higher plane of devotion.

If God had not been present with them in battle, then one way to guarantee His presence, they thought, might be to bring His ark into the camp. For many, confidence in the presence of the ark was a form of fetishism—the ultimate good luck charm. Magical potency was believed to dwell in the object itself. "The people sent to Shiloh" (4:4). There is no hint that they inquired whether it was proper for the ark to be carried into battle or whether God had any instructions for them as they faced this unequal struggle (it is of interest to note the practice of Moses, Joshua, and the judges in this regard). In their superstitious fear they simply demanded that ark, and evidently Eli was powerless to block its departure from the sanctuary. Of course, the priests had to accompany the ark just as they did during the period of desert wandering. Thus wicked and condemned Hophni and Phinehas went with the ark to the battlefront.

What a perfect setup for catastrophe! An idolatrous people who had largely turned their backs on Yahweh deserved His punishment. The army of the people of God was going into battle with no particular instruction of God and with greater trust in a piece of religious furniture than in the God whose presence it symbolized. The priests who accompanied the ark had been repudiated by God and marked for judgment.

When the ark arrived in the camp, the Hebrews shouted so vociferously that the earth itself reverberated (4:5). Their clamor probably was both a shout of joy and a battle cry. Some of them no doubt conjured up visions of the kind of victories Israel had enjoyed in the days of Moses and Joshua. And, like their enemies, many of these soldiers superstitiously must have believed that the power of deity was inseparably linked with a tangible representation of Him.

The commotion was so great in the Hebrew camp that at least Philistine scouting parties or advance guards could hear it. And under the circumstances, Israelite security probably was not so tight as to prevent penetration of the camp's perimeter, or at least inquiry from some Hebrew scouting party about what was going on. Panic seized the Philistine camp. Even if the Hebrews were not superstitious about the ark, the Philistines were; to them the presence of the ark symbolized God's physical presence. And even though generations had passed since the Hebrew conquest of Canaan, Philistine conviction of the power of Yahweh to perform miracles on behalf of Israel at the time of the Exodus and subsequently filled them with consternation. How they knew about God's doings in that earlier period is not stated, nor is it germane to the account to explain that detail. Philistine polytheistic orientation is clear from the plurals used in 4:8. Though the ten plagues did not take place "in the wilderness," from a Philistine perspective such a view was not especially erroneous. The Hebrews had lived in Goshen, at the edge of the wilderness, and God continued to do all sorts of miraculous things for them during the forty years of wilderness wandering.

With their backs to the wall, so to speak, and facing probable enslavement, the Philistines sought to inspire one another and fought with the courage of despair. The outcome was a resounding defeat for the Hebrews with a reported casualty figure of thirty thousand, the loss of the ark, and the deaths of Hophni and Phinehas. Some doubt the large numbers given for the armies and casualties in the historical books of the Old Testament, but there is no need to be particularly skeptical when we understand the nature of the warfare described. It was common that when a town or an area was threatened during the days of the conquest of Canaan, the period of the judges, or the monarchy, all the able-bodied men turned out—including the older teen-agers. Thus the numbers involved were considerably swollen. Then, precisely because most of those engaged in conflict were not disciplined soldiers, casualties frequently were excessive; and if an enemy was put to flight, the confusion or the rout often was total.

Sometimes, under conditions of defeat like this, and especially during the days of Assyrian and Babylonian conquest later, Hebrews might question whether God was able to save His people. Numerous passages indicate that He always had the power to do so but that He might not choose to do so if He sought to execute judgment for spiritual waywardness. In such cases He might run the risk of leading the enemies of Israel to believe that He was powerless. But ultimately He vindicated His name; and in this instance the Philistines were absolutely clear about Yahweh's superiority to their gods, as subsequent events were to demonstrate.

b) *Effect of the tidings at Shiloh* (4:12–21)

A Benjamite (rabbinic tradition says he was Saul) ran from the battlefield to Shiloh with his clothes torn and earth on his head—signs of mourning for the dead or a national catastrophe (cf. Josh. 7:6). Perhaps he was so intent on delivering news of the defeat and so overwhelmed with the tragedy that he ran right past blind Eli, who sat waiting "by the road" (4:13). "Deeply troubled about the ark," which had been taken off to battle without the command of God, Eli had positioned himself where he could most easily learn what had happened. Possibly "the gate" (v. 18) at which Eli sat was the main gate of the city where officials commonly gathered to do business and render judgment. Or possibly he sat at the gate of the temple, in which case the messenger would not have passed him on the way into town but subsequently would have delivered his personal message (vv. 15–18) at the temple precinct. In any event the runner broke the news to the townsfolk first, and the whole city cried out in terror. When Eli inquired about the tumult, the Benjamite came hurrying to him with the information he sought.

The sacred historian vividly described the scene. The aged judge and priest, now ninety-eight, sat on a stool without a back by the gate. He was blind—"his eyes were set" (4:15) from paralysis of the optic nerves—and he was very overweight. He was greatly agitated by a combination of fear for the safety of the ark and apprehension over the uproar throughout the town. The messenger came running to Eli and blurted out four devastating particulars in an ascending scale: the Israelite army had fled in panic; it had sustained great casualties; Hophni and Phinehas had been killed; and the ark had been captured. The shock of the rapid-fire recounting of disaster threw the aged priest into a state of shock. He had been somewhat prepared for the death of his sons by two previous announcements, but the loss of the ark was more than he could bear. Perhaps due to fainting or suffering a stroke, he fell over backward; and the weight of his body broke his neck and he died. The historian added that Eli had judged Israel forty years (4:18).

Judgment of Eli's house continued. His daughter-in-law, wife of Phinehas, was about to give birth to a child. The shock of the multiple catastrophe of the death of her father-in-law and husband and the seizure of the ark threw her into premature labor. As she lay dying and realized she had given birth to a son, she gasped out that his name should be

Ichabod (meaning "inglorious" or "no glory") because the "glory had departed" (literally, "gone into exile", cf. Ezek. 10:18 at the time of the
Babylonian exile) with the loss of the ark. The women attending her tried
to cheer her with news of the birth of her son, but she was too far gone to
respond.

   c) *Devastation wrought by the ark* (5:1–12)

Some Hebrews may have concluded that Yahweh was incapable of
protecting them against the Philistines, and Philistines generally may
have believed that they and their gods were able to overcome Yahweh.
However, subsequent events were to prove just the opposite. After the
victory in the vicinity of Aphek, the Philistines took the ark as one of the
trophies of war to Ashdod, presumably their capital. This city was located
thirty-three miles west of Jerusalem and about three miles from the
Mediterranean. On their arrival at Ashdod, they naturally deposited the
ark in the temple of Dagon, probably as a votive offering to their god, who
had given them the victory over Yahweh and the Hebrews.

Dagon, the father of Baal, was a vegetation deity—not a fish god as
used to be thought. Dagon was worshiped in Babylonia as early as 2200
B.C. and at Ras Shamra in Syria by 2000 B.C. He was also a member of the
Phoenician pantheon and was worshiped elsewhere in Palestine at Beth
Shan, according to 1 Chronicles 10:10. The Philistines maintained at least
one more temple to Dagon at Gaza, where Samson had won a great
victory over them (Judg. 16:23).

Having placed the ark in the holy of holies of the temple of Dagon at
Ashdod, the Philistines found the image of their god fallen prostrate
before the ark the very next morning. They were not willing to admit that
anything but some rumbling of the earth or an accident had caused the
statue to fall; so they put it back in place. The next morning Dagon was
again fallen prostrate before the ark, this time in a mutilated condition.
The torso faced the ark, and the head and hands lay in a slightly different
direction on the threshold, where they easily might be trodden on by
anyone entering the temple. Henceforth those who entered the temple
did not tread on the threshold but stepped over it so as not to defile the
place where pieces of their god had lain. Thus not only was Dagon
humiliated before Yahweh at a given moment, buy also the memory of
that humiliation was perpetuated for generations thereafter.

But God did not stop with total humiliation of the chief Philistine deity.
His "hand was heavy upon the people" (5:6), oppressing them as would a
ruling caste (cf. Judg. 1:35). He "ravaged them" (5:6 NASB; "brought devastation on them," NIV; the same verb is used for the destruction of vines
and fig trees in Hos. 2:12). And He afflicted them with "tumors" (5:6), or
"plague-boils," in the groin (cf. v. 9). Evidently rodents were involved in
spreading a kind of bubonic plague (cf. 6:4–5, 17–18). Soon the people of
the whole vicinity of Ashdod, seeing the agricultural base of their

economy eroding and writhing in agony from the plague, determined to rid themselves of the ark. A conclave of the princes of the Philistines counseled sending the ark to Gath. Possibly in this way it could be determined whether the sufferings of the Ashdodites arose from the ark of Yahweh and whether Yahweh sought to levy some special judgment against them.

The location of Gath is somewhat uncertain, but probably it is to be identified with Tell es-Safi, twenty-one miles due west of Bethlehem. When the ark arrived in Gath, it brought the same kind of destruction and suffering as at Ashdod. The people of Gath sent the ark on to Ekron, also of uncertain location but probably to be identified with a site ten to fifteen miles east of Ashdod. There the story was the same as at the other two Philistine towns. But in this case there is a clear indication of numerous deaths (5:11–12); and it must be assumed that widespread death accompanied the plague elsewhere as well. This whole account reads like a triumphal march of Yahweh. Before Him pagan gods were powerless to protect either themselves or their worshipers. Though Yahweh might use pagan people to punish sinful Israelites, an Israelite defeat should not be construed to indicate divine impotence.

d) *Return of the ark to Israel* (6:1–7:2)

Finally the Philistines had taken just about all they could bear. After the ark had been in their possession for seven months, many were willing to relinquish this rich prize of war. But apparently opinion on the matter was still divided; not all were convinced that their calamities had come from the hand of the God of Israel. So the priests and diviners or soothsayers were called for counsel. They recommended a course of action that could at the same time determine whether Yahweh was responsible for their woes and could appease Him or indemnify Him for wrongs done to Him in the abduction of the ark.

What they suggested put God to a severe test to prove Himself; it was quite unthinkable that it would work. Their instructions included provision of a new cart on which the ark could be transported. It was to be drawn by two cows that had calved and never been yoked, rather than by male oxen. The calves of these cows were to be penned up at home. Then the cows were to be sent on their way to take the ark back into Israelite territory. Under normal circumstances the cows would rebel against being yoked and possibly jump around and break the cart. They would need to be driven to get them to move and to show them where to go, and they would seek to return to their calves instead of going in the opposite direction. Unwittingly the priests gave God an opportunity to display His soveriegn power before pagan Philistines. And it may even be argued that He put the details of this test in their minds so He could manifest His glory among the Philistines. Of course, the priests also gave instructions concerning an offering for Yahweh.

This offering was to be reckoned as a "guilt" (6:3; "trespass," KJV) offering—an indemnity or reparations—to appease an angered god who had been wronged. The recommendation to present golden tumors and golden rats followed the ancient principle that like cures like. The tumors stood for the disease they suffered and the rats for the rodents that had been spreading the plague and destroying property. Thus the plea was that by this valuable gift they would "give glory to the God of Israel" (6:5 NASB, i.e., recognize His power as God) and would specifically beg that He terminate the plague and destruction among them. The "five" (6:4) tumors and rats represented the five Philistine towns (v. 18). Though verse 4 mentions five models of tumors and five of rats, verse 18 implies that there may have been more than five rats, because they represented not only the five major cities but also the "towns" and "villages." The priests had recommended five golden rats; but since these rodents had infested the entire region, evidently the smaller towns also sent offerings. Presumably the suffering from the tumors had occurred only in the major centers where the ark had gone.

Verse 6 need not be taken as an evangelical-sounding exhortation by Philistine priests to repentance before Yahweh on the part of a reluctant Philistine citizenry. It may only refer to a residual fear of Yahweh that existed in Canaanite memory from the days of the Exodus and wilderness wandering and an encouragement to stop opposing any measure that might appease Him, if indeed He was responsible for what had been going on. It was not unusual for ancient peoples to fear the acts of gods of other peoples, even of their enemies. The decision to send the ark to Beth Shemesh, some ten miles east of Ekron and fifteen miles west of Jerusalem, probably was reached because it was the nearest Israelite town to Ekron. Moreover, Beth Shemesh was a Levitical city (Josh. 21:16); and the Levites especially were custodians of the tabernacle.

The Philistines did exactly as they were instructed. A "new cart" (6:7) was necessary to show proper respect for deity; it was hardly appropriate to use an old cart formerly employed for a variety of secular purposes and stained with all sorts of produce. The carrying of the ark on a cart was forbidden, but Philistine ignorance of instructions given to the Hebrews could be forgiven. When the Philistines turned the cows loose, wonder of wonders, the animals took the road straight to Beth Shemesh, never wandering from the path. Their "lowing" (6:12) is usually taken as a desire for their calves as they moved away from them under divine compulsion. The "lords of the Philistines" (6:12), the princes of the five Philistine towns, followed the cart, probably not so much to present their tribute as to prevent any manipulation of the venture and to gain firsthand evidence of what happened. They trooped behind the cart all the way to the edge of Beth Shemesh.

When the ark arrived at Beth Shemesh, probably in May, nearly the entire population was out in the Valley of Sorek, which lay to the north of the town, harvesting the spring wheat crop. The people of Beth Shemesh welcomed the ark with an outburst of joy. And when the cows stood still by a large rock in the field of a certain Joshua, the Beth Shemites had a natural altar on which to make a sacrifice of thanksgiving for the ark's safe return and materials for such a sacrifice. They chopped up the cart for firewood and used the cows as sacrificial animals—as whole burnt offerings. In addition the people made "whole-offerings" and "shared-offerings" (6:15 NEB) of their own to God. The former were completely consumed and involved renewed consecration to God; the latter were partially burned, with the rest eaten in a sacrificial meal, and bespoke a renewal of living fellowship with God. After the five rulers of the Philistines had witnessed "all this" (6:16 NIV), a tremendous confirmation of the power of God and authentication of His recent acts among them, they returned to Ekron that same day. There is no indication whether the Philistines feared for their lives while they were among the Hebrews or whether the Hebrews feared some stratagem; nor is there a hint that there was any verbal exchange between them.

Shortly the Hebrews were also to have their problems with the ark. Verse 19 describes God's judgment on the people of Beth Shemesh, but complete accuracy of the text is hard to determine. The Jerusalem Bible and the New English Bible follow manuscripts that saw judgment as falling on the sons of Jeconiah: "Of the people of Beth-shemesh the sons of Jeconiah had not rejoiced when they saw the ark of Yahweh, and he struck" (JB). Other manuscripts and translations envision the judgment as resulting from a looking with profane curiosity at or into the ark (cf. KJV, NASB, NIV). This was specifically proscribed or warned against as fatal (Num. 4:20).

In any case the men of Beth Shemesh learned, like the Philistines, that holiness is dangerous. They exclaimed, "Who can stand in the presence of the LORD, this holy God?" (6:20 NIV). But then, instead of mending their ways, they decided that the easiest way to solve this problem was to get the ark (the special manifestation of the presence of God) out of their midst. There is a lesson here for the present generation of Christians, who seem largely to have forgotten the danger and the demands of the holiness of God in their rush to make Him intensely human. Both the Old and New Testaments are clear in their teaching that an infinitely holy God demands holiness on the part of His people (cf. Acts 5:1–11).

An additional problem with the text of verse 19 concerns the number of those judged. Two numbers stand next to each other in some versions: seventy and fifty thousand. The town of Beth Shemesh itself was small; and a large district hardly could have been involved in its sin, whatever that was. The usual conclusion is that a copyist's error has crept in here and that only seventy were struck down. The great first-century Jewish historian Josephus supports seventy as accurate (*Antiquities* 6. 1. 4).

The men of Beth Shemesh may have had strategic considerations as well as spiritual issues in mind when they wanted to move the ark. If so, their thought was to move it away from the Philistine border to Kiriath Jearim, a place higher in the Judean hills, about ten miles northeast of Beth Shemesh and about nine or ten miles west of Jerusalem. The men of Kiriath Jearim responded to the invitation to come and take charge of the ark. They brought it into the house of Abinadab and consecrated his son Eleazar, presumably a Levite, as its priest. The ark was destined to stay there for twenty years before the curtain rose on the biblical drama once more. The reason why the ark was not returned to Shiloh may be twofold: the site had been defiled and lost respect; and presumably the Philistines had destroyed it after the battle of Ebenezer or a little later. Excavations at Shiloh indicate that it was destroyed about the middle of the eleventh century B.C.

2. Samuel's revival ministry and Philistine defeat (7:3–17)

With rare exceptions (e.g., the story of Job), Scripture does not report in detail or with pathos the sufferings or difficult moments of individuals or groups. This passage runs true to form. Hardly even hinted at here are the indifference of the Hebrews to the ark in particular, the worship of Yahweh in general, their idolatrous condition, and their sufferings brought on by severe oppression at the hands of the Philistines. The narrator also passes over the emotions of a heartbroken Samuel as he agonized over his people deprived of a shepherd and who were callous and unresponsive to the claims of God.

Yet Samuel did not give up as he faced one of the most discouraging challenges ever to confront a servant of God. Evidently he doggedly persevered all during those years, trying to get his people to turn to God. His efforts finally began to bear fruit. After twenty years of spiritual malaise, "there was a movement throughout Israel to follow the LORD" (7:2 NEB). This movement presumably was brought on not so much by a pricking of their consciences as by Philistine oppression.

As this seeking after God began to manifest itself, Samuel urged the people to demonstrate the sincerity of their repentance by forsaking their idol worship and committing themselves unreservedly to God. It was often said during World War II that "there are no atheists in foxholes." Plagued by war and oppression, people frequently are scared into a quasi-genuine faith in God. Samuel pleaded with his people to make their turning to God a truly authentic experience. He wanted them to give evidence of their repentance by appropriate fruits or conduct (Luke 3:8). In begging his people to abandon their idols in order to demonstrate true repentance, Samuel was preaching a message close to the observation of the apostle Paul that the Thessalonians had "turned to God from idols"

(2 Thess. 1:9), where "turned" translates a word elsewhere rendered "repent"). They had repudiated their idols and committed themselves totally to God—exactly what Samuel was asking his hearers to do.

Samuel's exhortation was accompanied by a promise that after personal and national reformation God "will deliver you out of the hand of the Philistines (7:3). The cycle reflected here is essentially the same as in the Book of Judges: apostasy is followed by foreign oppression, and that in turn by repentance, divine rescue or relief, and a period of freedom from bondage.

"Ashtoreths" in the plural is synonymous with "goddesses"; in the singular it refers to the Greek Astarte or the Babylonian Ishtar, a goddess of fertility and war whose worship involved licentious rites. Baalim is another plural for pagan deities, but in the singular it applies to the supreme male Canaanite god, the sky god who fertilized the land. His worship too might be accompanied by licentious rites.

The Hebrew people responded positively to Samuel's call to turn from their apostasy. Then Samuel summoned them for a public confession and reaffirmation of faith at Mizpah, identified by most scholars with Tell en-Nasbeh, eight miles north of Jerusalem. "All Israel" (7:5) evidently does not mean that all the millions of Israelites were to gather at that small town—an impossible feat—but that at least their official representatives were to convene. Samuel's intention to "intercede" (v. 5) for his people showed that Old Testament prophets served not merely as heralds of divine truth but also as priests. Symbolically and by specific pronouncement the people confessed their sin. The pouring out of water was a repentance ritual symbolic of contrition and a need for cleansing. Fasting also had the connotation of sorrow.

In acting as "judge" (7:6), Samuel was not administering punishment, nor pronouncing censure, nor granting absolution to the penitent. Rather, through his intercession for Israel he attained forgiveness and the renewal of God's favor. With His people in a right relationship to Him once more, God was free to vindicate their rights (another meaning of the verb "judge") or deliver them. Samuel won that vindication and deliverance for his people by his leadership role.

Apparently the Philistines sought to take advantage of Israel's preoccupation with a religious observance (as Arabs did in the Yom Kippur War of 1973), and possibly resolved to launch a preemptive strike because they interpreted the Hebrew gathering as preparation for war. Whether or not the Philistines believed that the Hebrews were getting ready to rebel against them, spiritual revival among the Hebrews would put them in a better position to throw off the Philistine yoke. After all, oppression had plagued the Hebrews because of their waywardness. Fear gripped the Hebrews as reports of a Philistine advance reached the holy convocation. Unprepared for war, they begged Samuel not to stop crying out to God on their behalf. Though not a priest, Samuel offered a lamb as a whole burnt offering, thus representing the total consecration of the people to their God.

The account of God's response is dramatic and vivid. While Samuel was offering the sacrifice and as the Philistines were advancing against the Hebrews, Yahweh split the heavens with a terrorizing thunderstorm that threw the Philistine army into complete panic. Perhaps He struck down many of them with bolts of lightning. God defeated the Philistines before the Hebrews had a chance to strike a blow. All the Hebrews had to do was launch a mopping-up exercise. Emboldened by the turn of events, they rushed against the confused and fleeing foe with such success that the Philistines "no longer encroached on the territory of Israel" (7:13 NEB). Evidently this does not mean the Philistines made no effort to recover lost territory or supremacy. The following clause indicates that such attacks did take place, but they were doomed to failure because of divine intervention.

Verse 14 probably does not imply that the important Philistine towns of Ekron and Gath fell to the Israelites but only that borderlands adjacent to them did. Moreover, resurgent Israelite power was so impressive that the Amorites, the most powerful of the Canaanite tribes, did not greatly trouble the Hebrews either during the rest of the days of Samuel's leadership. Beth Car and Shen are otherwise unknown. Ebenezer ("stone of help") signified that God graciously helped the Israelites in their hour of need (this place is not to be confused with the town of Ebenezer in 1 Sam. 4:1).

From the time that Samuel's ministry was so dramatically vindicated at Mizpah, he evidently exercised the judgeship or rule over the nation. This leadership function was to continue along with his prophetic office the rest of his life. To make it possible for more of the people to have direct access to his ministry, he established a judicial circuit, including Bethel, Gilgal, Mizpah, and Ramah. Whether the Gilgal in the Jordan Valley or the one southwest of Shiloh is entended must be left open to question. Problems attend locating the other towns also, but the generalization can be made that they were only a few miles apart in the hills of Ephraim in central Palestine. Therefore, even though Samuel may have been respected at a greater distance, his itinerant ministry did not take him to Galilee, Trans-Jordan, or farther afield than the northern edge of Judah. That his authority was accepted widely is clear from the next chapter, in which his sons acted as his deputies at Beersheba in the south and "all the elders of Israel" (8:4) came to him with the request for a king.

For Further Study

1. Do a character study on Samuel, noting his personal traits, factors contributing to his personal development, and the results of his characteristics and/or his actions.

2. Analyze Hannah's song in 1 Samuel 2:1-10 to see what it reveals about the character of God and the attitudes of Hannah toward God.

3. Make a study of marriage in the Bible to discover what support there is for the monogamous position.

4. Study the ill effects of polygamy as seen in the lives of Elkanah, Jacob, and Solomon.

5. In a Bible dictionary or encyclopedia, study the Philistines as to their origin, history, and religion.

Chapter 2

The Rise of Saul
(1 Samuel 8:1–15:35)

A. Israel's Demand for a King (8:1–22)

As Samuel grew older, he no longer had the vigor to shoulder the entire load of ruling Israel. But sharing responsibility with his sons proved to be no solution, for evidently they never fully subscribed to the spiritual and ethical ideals of their father. When they assumed judicial responsibilities at Beersheba, some fifty miles southwest of Jerusalem, the strictures of their father's watchful eye no longer controlled them. They took bribes and perverted justice and thus provided the Hebrews with an excuse for requesting a change in government. This passage once more points up the truth that however saintly and effective believers may be in the conduct of their ministry, they cannot pass on spriituality to their offspring. Each new generation must make its own commitment to God and His standards of conduct. No new generation inherits spiritual life along with physical life.

Using Samuel's advancing age and his sons' degenerate behavior as the bases for their request, the elders of Israel came as representatives of the people to plead for the institution of a monarchy. Of course, Samuel was upset over the elders' vote of no confidence in his administration, but he did not answer their charges. His concern centered rather on their desire for a king and the implications of that request for the divine order of things in Israel. Not knowing how to respond, Samuel sought God's face for wisdom and comfort. God's reply was that Israel was not really rejecting Samuel. Instead, lack of confidence in God Himself had led them to reject an invisible God-king and ask for a visible king. Their impatience with their powerlessness as a nation had goaded them to want a king like those of other peoples—one who could lead them into war and make something of them as a people. They failed to realize that their weakness resulted from disobedience to God. Had they been faithful to God, an earthly visible king would have been unnecessary.

It should be clear, however, that Israel was only demanding a change in executive headship. They were not repudiating God's moral code.

Moreover, they wanted a king whom God would sanction and whom Samuel would anoint. Furthermore, the request for a king had been predicted hundreds of years before and actually had been sanctioned in the law. In fact, some commentators argue that their request so closely resembles the original Hebrew of Deuteronomy 17:14 that the elders had Moses' provisions in mind. Presumably this was the time for the kingship to be instituted because God acceded to their request. A further indication of the degree of Hebrew obedience to God is seen in the willingness of the people to go home and await God's time and method of choosing their king (8:22).

God granted the demand for a king but instructed Samuel to warn the people about what sort of person he would be. In a word he would be an Oriental style of absolute monarch who would exercise the right to use persons and property for his own purposes as he saw fit. He would be guilty of personal aggrandizement and rapaciousness. And since ostentatious regal courts and military establishments do not come cheaply, he would exact heavy taxes.

Specifically, verses 11–17 warn of at least five actions to be expected of the king. (1) Conscription for military service (vv. 11–12). (2) The exercise of eminent domain: sovereign power over all property within the state, by which it can appropriate private property for public use (v. 14). (3) Corvée or conscript labor—obligation imposed on inhabitants of a district to perform services (vv. 12, 16). Sometimes it is a tax in the form of labor. (4) Impressment of persons—to force them into public service, to seize or take for public use (vv. 13, 16). (5) Heavy taxation (vv. 15, 17).

The elders or representatives of Israel repudiated the warnings about the monarchy. They insisted on a visible "king" (8:19) in a permanent institution of monarchy as opposed to a temporary magistracy directed by an unseen governor. Moreover, they wanted a standing army under his command to deal with the threats of neighboring states. It was convenient to forget how often God had fought their battles for them when they were unable to fight their own. Though they had insisted on a king "like all the other nations" (8:5), God would not grant them that wish. He would insist on a king who was different: reverent toward God and just toward His people. Failure in either respect would bring removal from office, termination of one's dynasty, or other forms of judgment.

B. The Choice and Coronation of Saul (9:1–10:27)

How long the Hebrews had to wait for the choice of a king is not clear. There was no emergency that required haste. The elders of Israel had the commitment of God's prophet, and thus of God Himself, that the monarchy would be established; therefore they were content to allow events to unfold in due course. The patience of the Orient does not require immediate or rapid implementation of promises made.

But the sacred historian proceeded immediately to introduce the person who was to become Israel's first king. He was from a prominent family, as the rather elaborate genealogy was meant to imply. The genealogy is only partial, however; additional names in the pedigree may be found elsewhere (1 Sam. 10:21; 14:51; 1 Chron. 7:6, 8; 9:35; Gen. 46:21). Saul was also from a family of "substance" or "property" (9:1). The KJV description of his father, Kish, as "a mighty man of power" (9:1) is misleading. It implies that he had great physical prowess, but the Hebrew original means that he had the power in his community that comes with extensive possessions. Another important point about Saul's heritage was that he came from the tribe of Benjamin, the smallest of the tribes of Israel. Therefore his elevation to kingship would stir none of the jealousies that might arise from membership in one of the more prominent tribes.

As to his personal qualifications, Saul was a young man "in the prime of life" (9:2), but it is impossible to be more definite than that about his age. If one follows some later manuscripts of the Septuagint translation of 1 Samuel 13:1, he was thirty when he began to reign. Some conclude that he was forty or older at this time because his grown son, Jonathan, appeared on the scene soon after his anointing to be king. But it is not clear how much time elapsed between 1 Samuel 9 and 13:2, and Jonathan may have been very young when he launched his first military action. Very young men have often been formidable warriors. For example, Clovis became king of the Franks at fifteen and apparently soon thereafter led his warriors into battle to establish Frankish power in Western Europe. Charles XII of Sweden, the "Alexander of the North," became king at fifteen and began his extensive military campaigns at eighteen. "Goodly . . . there was no better" (9:2) may refer to moral qualities, but the context suggests physical appearance. Hence, the text may be paraphrased to say, "There was none more handsome than he." And he was a head taller than anyone else.

Having introduced the person of the king, the writer next proceeds to the circumstances that put him in touch with Samuel and thus led to his proclamation as king. The narrative begins on a purely naturalistic plane, but soon it is evident that God sovereignly and supernaturally had been ordering all the details of this episode in Saul's life. God spoke directly to Samuel to announce Saul's coming and to command Samuel to anoint him king (9:16). When the two met on the following day, God confirmed to Samuel that Saul was the one whose coming He had predicted (9:17). Then, presumably, God also revealed Saul's need to Samuel before Saul could report it to the seer (9:20). After Saul's anointing to kingship, Samuel announced additional supernaturally discerned details—all of which came to pass. There were the two men who told Saul of his father's worry over his son's extended absence (10:2), the three men who presented him with bread (10:4), and the descent of the Holy Spirit on him to sweep him up in an ecstatic experience (10:6). The fulfillment of these predictions served as confirmation of God's choice of Saul.

The story of Saul's meeting with Samuel had a rather commonplace beginning. Some of Kish's she-asses had strayed, under what circumstances is not clear, nor is it important. Kish decided to send his son Saul to look for them in the company of "one of the servants" (9:3), an indication that there were several servants and that the family was at least relatively well-to-do. Evidently the pair set out from Gibeah, Saul's hometown, located three miles north of the present Damascus Gate in Jerusalem. Their search took them northward into the hill country of Ephraim and through several districts located in the central part of Palestine subsequently called Samaria. It is not possible to locate precisely the places mentioned in 9:4. Presumably the pair started out in a northwesterly direction and made a great loop to the southeast and then came back home.

As the days passed Saul began to fear that his father would begin to worry about his safety; so he determined to return home. But the servant, not wanting the mission to end in failure, suggested one last effort to locate the animals. They were now in the region of Zuph (Samuel's home territory), and the servant thought they ought to talk to the prophet about their problem. Evidently the servant's attitude was "he knows everything." Possibly the servant even ascribed to him some clairvoyant powers. At any rate the pair had been on a long, unfruitful journey and their provisions were gone (9:7); nothing was to be lost by this last-ditch effort. The old platitude "man's extremity is God's opportunity" was to be proved again. A fruitless search for the she-asses led to the finding of a kingdom.

From the language used in verses 6–7 it is clear that Samuel was not known to either Saul or his servant. Evidently Samuel's itinerant ministry did not take him to the vicinity of Gibeah, and probably Saul never moved far from home. It is also evident that Samuel was not at his hometown of Ramah but somewhere else along his circuit, for all indications in the context point to Samuel's officiating as a visiting priest. For example, the city is referred to as the place where the man of God "was" (9:10), not "dwelt." And the girls reported "he has just come to our town today" (9:12 NIV) to officiate at a sacrifice.

The need to present some small gift to the man of God caused Saul momentary consternation because he had nothing to give; however, his servant produced a piece of silver (v. 8). This was silver by weight, for the first coinage did not appear until several hundred years later—in western Asia Minor. The value of the gift cannot be calculated in current equivalency, but Saul judged it to be adequate for the occasion. The pair then set out for the nearby town and the expected meeting with the prophet.

The parenthetical expression in verse 9 has given rise to considerable discussion. At the minimum it may be said that a seer was one who was favored with visions of God or from God. A prophet could foretell the future and had the special responsibility of communicating the word of God. It may be argued that although the prophetic voice was heard during the days of Moses, it was rarely heard in the times of the judges (1 Sam. 3:1). In the days of Samuel, however, when the schools of the prophets arose and the spirit of prophecy more often fell on men, there was a tendency to unite the function of seer and prophet in one person and to use the terms interchangeably. But the common term beginning in Samuel's day was "prophet."

Saul and his servant now ascended the slope toward the city gate. Palestinian towns normally were walled and were perched on defensible heights near a water supply and adequate farmland. As the pair advanced they met some girls coming out of town to get the daily water supply for their families from the community well. The time must have been toward evening, for normally the water supply was laid in for the following day at that time. On inquiry as to whether the seer was in town, Saul and his servant were informed that he was and that he was about to go out to the high place to preside over a sacrificial meal. They were urged to hurry because Samuel was close behind the girls and the two visitors would no doubt meet him near the city gate.

That in fact happened; Samuel was coming out as they were going in. Saul did not recognize Samuel because the prophet wore no insignia or special dress to set him apart from others. But Samuel recognized Saul, because God at that moment revealed to the prophet that this was the one whom he was to anoint king of Israel. When Saul inquired of Samuel about directions to the seer's house, Samuel identified himself and invited Saul to participate in the sacrificial meal and to spend the night with him. Then he informed Saul that the she-asses had been found, and the added note appears that the search had been going on for three days. "On whom is all the desire of Israel" (9:20 KJV) is a cryptic reference to the royal honor that awaited Saul, and his answer showed that he caught its significance. He answered with proper modesty, observing that his family was insignificant among the families of Benjamin, smallest of the twelve tribes.

Without any further recorded protestations, Samuel led Saul and his servant into the "hall" (9:22) adjacent to the sanctuary where a communal meal was about to be shared after a peace offering. About thirty invited guests were assembled, and Samuel ushered Saul and his servant to the seats of honor. Then he instructed the cook to bring the priest's portion, the shoulder (the right leg), and set it before Saul. What had been planned as a special communal meal shared with town elders and blessed by the presence of the prophet turned into a dinner in honor of Israel's future king. After the meal Samuel and his guests returned to town; and the prophet had a long talk with Saul on the flat roof of the house where he lodged. One can imagine that they conversed about spiritual and political questions, and especially about the nature of the kingdom soon to be established.

Then Saul slept on the housetop, probably in a booth. At dawn Samuel awoke him so he would have all the hours of daylight for traveling. As the prophet walked with the pair at the beginning of their journey, he requested that the servant go on alone so he could give Saul a "message from God" (9:27 NIV). What the servant thought by now must be left to conjecture. Evidently he had heard the conversation of verses 20 and 21, and he must have wondered at all the special attention during the fellowship meal. Perhaps events of the visit with Samuel helped to prepare him to be a loyal servant to the first king of Israel.

With the servant out of sight, Samuel proceeded to anoint Saul with oil and to kiss him. The anointing was a sort of investiture of office and a symbol of the endowment of the Spirit of God. Now the monarchy took its place alongside the priesthood as a divine institution; and through it would come the blessings of the sovereign God-king for civil government, as through the priesthood came the blessings of God for spiritual and ethical government. Samuel's kiss frequently is considered to be a token of homage; but probably it was merely a sign of affection and support because bowing, kneeling, and prostration were the common ways of demonstrating fealty in the ancient Near East.

Then, promptly, Samuel sought to prove the truth of Saul's anointing to kingship by giving him three signs. First, he would meet two men "near Rachel's tomb, at Zelzah on the border of Benjamin" (10:2 NIV). They would inform him that that she-asses had been found and his father was now worried about him. Evidently Rachel's tomb was not then located at the currently traditional site two miles north of Bethlehem but at some point much farther north. Some would put it near Ramah of Benjamin, about five miles north of Jerusalem; and others would put it in the vicinity of Jerusalem. The exact site cannot be fixed.

Then, in the vicinity of the "oak" (10:3; "tree of Tabor," NIV), Saul was to have another encounter. Again the location is uncertain, but evidently the tree stood a very short distance from Rachel's tomb and thus probably just north and west of Jerusalem. Certainly, Mount Tabor (six miles southeast of Nazareth) is not referred to here. This time they would meet three men headed for the worship center at Bethel where they intended to offer a sacrifice. For the purpose they would have three kids for sacrifice, three loaves for the offering, and a skin full of wine for a libation. They would offer Saul and his servant each a "loaf," or "cake," on the order of modern Arab bread or a pancake.

Third, when the pair came near "the hill of God" or "Gibeath-Elohim" (10:5), commonly identified with Geba (1 Sam. 13:3), about six miles north of Jerusalem, they would meet a company of prophets coming down from the high place. These men would be in the grip of "prophetic rapture" or some sort of ecstatic experience produced by the Spirit of God. As Saul met them, this same spirit would seize him; and he would engage in some ecstatic behavior with them. Their musical instruments are identified as the psaltery or lute (an instrument with ten or twelve strings), a tambourine, flute or primitive clarinet, and harp or lyre.

But one must be careful not to emphasize outward phenomena. It is stated clearly that the "Spirit of the LORD" (10:6) would "rush upon" him or would "suddenly take possession" of him. Then he would be "changed" (10:6; "turned") into another man. The change would be catastrophic; the same term is used in the Hebrew text of Genesis 19:25 in reference to the destruction of Sodom and Gomorrah. Saul would be revolutionized or turned into something he was not previously. Not only would he have external experiences confirming his anointing to kingship, but also he would know internally and experientially that God was with him as he sensed a new energy and wisdom for the conduct of his office. Verse 7 teaches that whenever divine power came on him, Saul would know that God was with him, spurring him to action and guiding him in it.

At first glance, it appears that verse 8 is unrelated to Samuel's earlier comments to Saul. But evidently Samuel meant it to be a clear instruction for future action (at the second assembly at Gilgal, cf. 1 Sam. 13:8); and if more of Samuel's conversation were reported here, no doubt the connection would be more plain. The matter is clarified by looking at the order of events about to take place: occurrence of the announced signs, choice of Saul as king at Mizpah, the Ammonite war, renewal of the monarchy at Gilgal, and the actual start of Saul's reign as he began to fulfill his commission to destroy the Philistines (cf. 9:16). It was as Saul began the war with the Philistines that he summoned the forces to Gilgal and failed to wait for Samuel to offer sacrifice and issue divine instruction (1 Sam. 13:8).

As Samuel left Saul that morning, God "changed his [Saul's] heart" (10:9) or gave him a new disposition or a new courage to undertake the tasks before him. The three signs predicted occurred "on that day" (v. 9). However one plots Saul's itinerary, not more than a few hours of walking would have been required to experience all that Samuel had prophesied. Understandably, attention focuses on the third of the signs because that one was especially important to Saul's preparation for kingship and because it was the one that created such a stir among his acquaintances.

Evidently Saul's previous life was completely different from that of the prophets, and the change caused great wonderment. "Who is their father?" (10:12) may be understood in either a positive or negative way. Negatively put, it may refer to the prophets as an odd bunch who belong to no family but are flotsam that collect from anywhere. Positively, the question may imply that if the others did not receive the prophetic spirit by inheritance but by divine bestowal, then Saul may have obtained it by the same means. The meaning of the proverb "Is Saul also among the prophets?" (10:11) likewise is susceptible to two interpretations. It may record surprise at the appearance of one in a role that is strange to him or ridicule of one well placed in life who finds himself in ecentric company.

After Saul's ecstatic experience ceased, he "came to the high place" (10:13). This is understood to mean a high place near his home where he met his uncle, or to refer to a place name, "Bamah" (meaning "high place"), adjacent to Gibeah, where his relatives lived. The NEB renders the passage "he went home." In any case Saul did arrive at home where his uncle engaged him in conversation about events of recent days. Saul told about looking for the lost animals but divulged nothing of the momentous events that had befallen him. Perhaps Samuel had assured him that God would arrange a public announcement of His choice of king. It would have been difficult for Saul to persuade the nation by himself of his divine choice and his credentials.

Soon Samuel did indeed arrange for a public presentation of Saul. He "summoned" (10:17) or commanded "the people," not merely the elders, but heads and/or representatives of tribes and families and households to gather at Mizpah about eight miles north of Jerusalem. There Samuel had previously led the people in confession of sin and a great victory over the Philistines (7:6, 11). Before proceeding to the choice of a king, Samuel once more reminded the people that their real Savior was God, and that they were rejecting Him in demanding a king to lead them. "Today" (10:19 NASB), though their disobedience in demanding a king had expressed itself earlier, it continued to be manifest in this solemn gathering. Then, implying that God had acceded to their wishes, Samuel instructed the people to "present yourselves before the LORD" (v. 19), i.e., to gather by the altar in order to begin the process of casting the sacred lot (cf. Josh. 7:16–18). The lot first fell on the tribe of Benjamin. Then, reference to intermediate steps being omitted, the lot finally fell on Saul.

But Saul was nowhere in evidence, probably finding it easier to be absent while the selection process was going on and not wishing to appear too eager. Either nervous excitement or modesty could have prompted him to act as he did. He was certainly not trying to avoid being chosen; he already knew God had put His hand on him. "They inquired . . . of the LORD" (10:22) as to Saul's whereabouts; that is, they probably sought help from the high priest, who then would employ the Urim and Thummim (cf. Exod. 28:30; Num. 27:21). When the answer came that Saul was hiding himself among the baggage of some of the assembled throng, he was promptly searched out.

Samuel then presented Saul as God's choice to be their king. There he stood in the prime of life, handsome and a head taller than anyone else. He was a man of good reputation in his community. And coming from the smallest tribe in Israel, he did not excite the jealousy and competition that would have arisen if he were from one of the major tribes. So a shout of acclamation reverberated through the assembled throng: "Let the king live," or more commonly, "Long live the king!"

But Samuel's duties did not end with the selection of a king. Though the people had desired a king "like" (8:5) the kings of nations around them, God had determined that the king of Israel was to be *different*. He was not to be an ordinary absolutist Oriental monarch but a sort of constitutional monarch. There were to be recognized divine and popular limits in his power. This fact comes clear from numerous references in the Old Testament (e.g., 2 Sam. 5:3; 2 Kings 11:17). In this case Samuel explained to the people the "ordinances (10:25 NASB; "regulations" NIV of the kingdom). Presumably he reiterated many of the points Moses had made earlier (Deut. 17:14–20), but no doubt expanded on them so that royal rights, privileges, and limitations were somewhat clearly defined. Then Samuel wrote these in a scroll and "deposited it before the LORD" (10:25), i.e. he put it in the custody of the priests as keepers of the archives. His task completed for the moment, Samuel sent the people home.

Saul had nowhere to go either but home. Israel had no capital nor government buildings. As Saul walked the five miles back to Gibeah, God put it on the hearts of some to accompany him. Regarding allegiance to be their conscientious duty, they became a sort of bodyguard and the nucleus of a standing army and government. And no doubt the many gifts of fealty and good wishes helped to finance Saul's operation in the early days of the kingdom. But some "scoundrels" (10:27; literally, "sons of Belial"; "troublemakers," NIV) were reluctant to accept Saul's divine appointment and brought him no gifts of fealty. Saul "kept silent" (v. 27), i.e. made no issue of the matter. He recognized the limitations of his power and was too wise to perpetrate internecine strife that might result from a demand for allegiance of all Israelites.

C. Saul's Accreditation by Victory (11:1–15)

What Saul needed for greater acceptance in Israel was an opportunity to act kingly—to demonstrate ability in warfare or public administration. The opportunity was provided by the threat of the Ammonites. Subjugated by Israel as a result of Jephthah's campaign (Judg. 11), the Ammonites had grown strong again and were threatening the city of Jabesh Gilead, a site about ten miles southeast of Beth Shan and about two miles east of the Jordan River. With no hope of rescue by Hebrews west of the Jordan, the townsfolk of Jabesh Gilead believed they would have to surrender to the Ammonites; and they sought a "treaty" (11:1; "covenant") that would give them the best possible terms. But the Ammonites demanded a terrible price—the blinding of all the men in the right eye. The reason for this requirement was twofold: to bring disgrace on Israel in retaliation for their subjugation to them, and incapacitation of the men so they could not fight, i.e., rebel.

Such a demand was too high a price for the Israelites to pay, and they begged for seven days of grace to obtain help. It is not unthinkable that the request should be granted because the Ammonites probably did not believe help would be forthcoming, and they wanted to avoid a siege of a walled city if possible. They could easily wait seven days for the inevitable to occur. Messengers from Jabesh Gilead immediately began to scurry among the tribes of Israel looking for support, and soon they arrived in Gibeah. The townspeople made a great lamentation, presumably not a mere expression of helplessness but a cry to God for help.

Some see evidence of no confidence in Saul in the fact that the messengers still viewed Israel as tribes and in the fact that they appealed to the townspeople of Gibeah instead of to Saul. But the conclusion might as easily be reached that people east of the Jordan did not yet know about the convocation at Mizpah. It is interesting to note that the Septuagint and some other ancient texts begin 1 Samuel 11:1 with the words "about a month later." The NEB follows this reading. If it is valid, this time reference easily explains the approach of the messengers.

As the commotion became general in Gibeah, Saul came in from working in the field. On being informed of the impending tragedy, he fell under the empowering of the Spirit of God (11:6). Earlier Saul had prophesied when the Spirit came on him (10:10–11); now "he burned with anger" (11:6 NIV) at the shame the Ammonites intended to bring on Israel. Then he performed the symbolic act of cutting up a yoke of oxen and sending the pieces throughout the tribes. He threatened to do the same as he had done to the oxen of anyone who failed to respond to the call for military action. The summons was a general one to "come out after Saul and . . . Samuel" (11:7). Not only did Saul still recognize the authority of Samuel, but he also needed all the sanctions he could get to pass the first test of his authority. The "terror" (11:7 or "fear") of Yahweh "fell on the people," impelling them to make a wholehearted response.

The mustering point was Bezek, a place in the hills on the western side of the Jordan opposite Jabesh Gilead. The number who responded is given as three hundred thousand from Israel and thirty thousand from Judah, some indication of the proportional size of the population of Judah and a hint of the future division between the tribes. The number sometimes is questioned or ridiculed as being too large. It is to be remembered, however, that these were not seasoned troops but a popular response of able-bodied men. Then the messengers from Jabesh Gilead were told to go home and promise deliverance on the morrow. Their tidings brought great joy to their townsmen.

Presumably on the night of the sixth day, the people of Jabesh Gilead informed the Ammonites that on the following day they would "come out" (11:10) to them. The Hebrew could mean to come out "against" or "in subjection to"—the ambiguity was convenient. Then, apparently, the Israelites marched all night from Bezek, fording the Jordan on the way. They formed three great divisions for the attack (cf. Judg. 7:16) and fell on the Ammonites "during the last watch of the night" (11:11 NIV), i.e., between three and six in the morning. The surprise was complete and the rout absolutely devastating. In the flush of victory Sauls' ecstatic supporters wanted to execute his opponents within Israel (cf. 10:27). But Saul possessed the spiritual perception to recognize that God had given the victory and the magnanimity to forgive and to prevent any bloodletting on his account.

Then Samuel seized on the opportunity to strengthen Saul's hand and to cement the bond of union that was growing among the Israelites. He called for a great convocation at Gilgal, just northeast of Old Testament Jericho, to renew the kingdom and celebrate Saul's coronation. Those gathered also made peace offerings to God. No doubt the offerings were followed by a great fellowship meal, as commonly occurred on such occasions. "All the Israelites rejoiced greatly" (11:15).

D. Samuel's Farewell Address (12:1–25)

But the celebration at Gilgal was a somber event as well, for Samuel chose this occasion to make his farewell address to the nation. It was appropriate for him to do so because actually he was resigning his magisterial authority as the new magistrate came on the scene. His speech began with a defense of his administration and continued with a reproof of Israelite waywardness and ingratitude. But especially he sought to make the point that popular expectations for success under the monarchy could be realized only as both king and people remained true to God.

Samuel started his address by observing that he had acceded to the request for a king. Now he "walks in front of you" (12:2) or is your "leader," both in military exploits and civil functions. "I have walked in front of you"; or "have been your leader until this day" (NIV). Samuel was old and was turning over the reins of administration.

As he did so he sought a defense of his official conduct in legal terms, speaking as if he were actually standing in a court of law. The Israelites were to "testify" (12:3) against him in the presence of the invisible and righteous God-king and His visible administrator of justice on earth, His anointed king. Samuel sought to clear himself in a variety of categories: appropriation of another's property, oppression, and miscarriage of justice as a result of bribery. The witnesses to or affirmations of his innocence in all three respects were unanimous. In fact, they went so far as to declare that they "found nothing" (12:5) in his hand, i.e., they gave him a clean bill of health as far as his public administration and his character were concerned. Therefore the intimation is made that Samuel was not to blame for the desire for a change of government. It was not because of his failures that they had desired a king; the fault lay in themselves.

In verse 5 God was a witness for Samuel's innocence. In verse 6 He begins to appear as a witness against the Israelites. In fact, wording to that effect occurs in the Septuagint translation; and the NEB, JB, and RSV phrase their translations on that basis: "And Samuel said to the people, 'The LORD is witness . . . now therefore stand'" (12:6–7 RSV). The great Deliverer of His people is a Witness against them and will "confront" or "plead" or "put the case against" (NEB) them, as if He were instituting a legal indictment.

In verses 7–12 Samuel recited a bit of history to demonstrate that "the LORD your God was your king" (12:12 NASB). The covenant God in grace had performed "righteous acts" (12:7) for them and their fathers. These included, first, deliverance from Egypt and safe guidance to Canaan and settlement there. Second, they involved numerous deliverances in Canaan from foes to which God had been forced to surrender them because of their apostasy. Oppressions singled out include: Sisera, commander-in-chief of the forces of King Jabin of Hazor (Judg. 4–5), the Philistines (Judg. 13–16), and the Moabites (Judg. 3).

In each case penitence had brought rescue, and God had raised up judges as deliverers. These included Jerub-Baal, or Gideon (Judg. 6–8), Barak ([Bedan in KJV is probably a copyist's error; the Septuagint and Syriac versions have Barak], Judg. 4–5), Jephthah (Judg. 10–12), and Samuel. Some have argued that Samuel would not have listed himself and prefer to follow a few inferior versions that list Samson here. But the Hebrew, Septuagint, and Latin Vulgate all agree on Samuel, and there is no convincing reason for accepting the reading of Samson. After all, Samuel had delivered the Israelites from the Philistines. And the mention of his own successes gave strength to the argument that God as King was continuing to lead His people in the present generation; therefore it was not necessary to have an earthly king to win battles against their enemies.

It is hard to know how to understand verse 12, because chapters 8 and 11 give no hint that the Ammonite threat had led to a demand for a king. It is true, however, that the request had come at a time of Ammonite incursion on Israelite territory; and victory over the Ammonites had been followed by the coronation of Saul. The main point at issue is that at that time in history they had demanded an earthly king, even though God as their King had been doing very well by them.

Now God had granted them their wish for a king. And even though in a sense they had rejected their God-king, He was still sovereign over them: "The LORD has set a king over you" (12:13). Moreover, God threatened punishment on people and king if they turned away from following Him (12:14–18). A people who were looking for a king to solve their problems and remove their calamities needed to be reminded that failure to follow Yahweh would bring His heavy hand of judgment on them "as upon your fathers" (12:15). Israel rarely could get it straight as to why they had troubles as a nation; it was not because they lacked a king.

Then, in order to give greater force to his words, Samuel called on God to perform a striking miracle—to send thunder and rain during wheat harvest. The time of harvest came in late May and early June, well within the dry season that lasted from April to October. Normally there was no rain during that period, even in western Palestine. Gilgal was east of the watershed in the Jordan Valley, and rainfall was much less frequent there; so a storm on this occasion would indeed be a phenomenon and would be regarded as evidence of divine omnipotence. Among other things this display of power demonstrated that the judgments of God might fall at any time. Thunder, regarded as the voice of God, brought panic to Israelites on this occasion as it had to the Philistines in 7:10.

The divine demonstration had its desired effect of producing a confession of failure from Israel and a request for intercession on their behalf. Samuel warned against the worship of false gods, because such an exercise was futile (12:20–21). He gave the assurance that God would not abandon His people, who were His by divine ordination and who would be preserved "for the sake of his great name (12:22). God had made His name great among the people of the East by doing marvelous things on behalf of His people. Though He might punish His people temporarily, His reputation would be destroyed on the earth if He abandoned them utterly. Samuel committed himself to a life of intercession for them and to responsible discipling of them (12:23).

In closing, the great prophet delivered one more exhortation to the people to unconditional service to God (in view of all He had done for them) and a warning that failure to do so would result in the people and their king being "swept away" (12:24–25). That judgment did indeed fall when the kingdom of Israel was "swept away," i.e., destroyed with a massive deportation of Israelites by the Assyrians in 723/22 B.C. The kingdom of Judah received like treatment at the hands of the Babylonians in 586 B.C.

E. Victories Over the Philistines (13:1–14:52)

With Saul's coronation accomplished and the reins of government turned over to him by Samuel, it was fitting that the new king should get on with the business for which he had been especially raised up, namely, the rescue of his people from the Philistines (1 Sam. 9:16). The sacred historian proceeded immediately to describe the contest between the Hebrews and their implacable foes. Actually there may have been a lapse of years during which Jonathan grew to maturity. Biblical history often is telescoped.

The introductory statement in 13:1 is difficult to evaluate. The Septuagint leaves it out altogether. The KJV reading of the verse, based on the Hebrew text, apparently concludes that the events of chapters 11 and 12 took place during Saul's first year, and the events about to take place occurred during his second year. Another reading, found in the Hexapla text of Origen of Alexandria (third century A.D.), states: "Saul was _____ years old when he began to reign, and he reigned _____ years over Israel." Those who adopt the latter differ on what numbers are to be inserted in the blanks. On the basis of Acts 13:21 and Josephus, Saul is given a forty-year reign. The first-century Jewish historian Josephus (*Antiquities* 6. 14.9) states that Saul reigned eighteen years before Samuel's death and twenty-two years afterward.

In any case chapter 13 clearly describes military preparations and military actions against the Philistines early in Saul's reign. Saul chose three thousand stalwarts as a sort of "palace guard" or a nucleus of the standing army. Of these, apparently one thousand were stationed with Saul at Micmash, about nine miles northeast of Jerusalem, and another thousand were under his jurisdiction around Bethel, about eleven miles north of Jerusalem. A third thousand were under the command of Jonathan at Gibeah, about three miles north of Jerusalem.

As noted in 1 Samuel 10:5 (NIV), there was a Philistine presence at Gibeah of God, about six miles northeast of Jerusalem, in the heartland of Benjamin. This Jonathan sought to eliminate. What he did there is not clear. The word commonly translated "garrison" (13:3) may mean garrison, or a resident administrator, or even some sort of Philistine monument. An attack on any of these would have been an affront to the Philistines and would have been taken as a signal that the Hebrews intended to throw off the Philistine yoke.

Therefore Saul sent out a general call for the Israelites to muster at Gilgal. And the Philistines also began to mobilize. The statistics given for the Philistine host, especially for the chariot corps, seem unreasonably large. There is a problem with the transcription of numbers in the Old Testament. Some texts of this verse give three thousand chariots, but even that figure is large; Solomon had only fourteen hundred chariots in his well-appointed military establishment (1 Kings 10:26). In any case the Philistine host was large, and the Israelites were no match for them. As the men went off to join Saul's army, the rest of the populace became absolutely terrified. Many hid themselves and others fled to the east side of the Jordan.

How many joined Saul at Gilgal is not clear, but they were a fearful lot and morale was low. As Samuel had instructed (1 Sam. 10:8), Saul waited for him seven days there. Meanwhile, the Philistines had occupied Saul's headquarters at Micmash and were assembling a large force there. As Saul's recruits melted away, he became desperate. When Samuel did not come, he determined to offer sacrifices himself and prepare for battle. No sooner had he completed the offering, however, than Samuel arrived and rebuked him for disobedience and lack of faith. For his lack of faith in an hour of crisis, Saul came under the condemnation of God and heard the sentenced from Samuel that his dynasty would not endure. God would choose a king "after his own heart" (13:14), and that man proved to be David. As subsequent events would demonstrate, however, this judgment did not mean that God would fail to give Saul great victories.

But for the moment the situation was desperate. Saul brought only six hundred men with him as he moved from Gilgal back toward Gibeah. There he joined Jonathan, who possibly still had at his disposal the thousand he had commanded there earlier (13:2). Presumably Saul and Jonathan stationed themselves at Gibeah, not only because it was their hometown, but also because Samuel had retired there (13:15). Divine resources were about all the Israelites had left. As they cringed in fear and waited for a devastating blow by Philistine forces, Philistine marauding parties moved almost at will from their camp at Micmash. Fanning out they carried off whatever moveable wealth they could find.

Not only were the Israelite soldiers few in number and demoralized, but they were also poorly armed. After the defeat of the Israelites in the days of Eli, the Philistines had kept them in subjection by preventing them from having access to iron weapons (13:19–21). The iron age came to Canaan about 1200 B.C., and iron weapons and utensils were proving themselves vastly superior to the old bronze equipment. The Philistines were determined to maintain both a metallurgical and military/political advantage over the Israelites by denying to them either products made from iron or knowledge of how to process it. Therefore, only Saul and Jonathan had "proper" weapons and body armor. That does not mean the Israelites had to fight with their bare hands, however. Their weapons ranged from crude clubs to deadly slings.

1. *Jonathan's surprise attack* (14:1–15)

As the stalemate continued between the Philistine and Israelite forces, Jonathan had a sudden inspiration to launch a surprise attack on the Philistine outpost guarding the pass between Micmash and Geba. The Philistines controlled the area north of the pass and the Israelites the territory south of it. The outpost to be attacked lay on the north of the pass at a point where side valleys intersected the main pass and created formidable crags on the north and south of the pass. Jonathan did not choose to move north and east out of Gibeah and skirt the pass on the north because that was a highly protected route, and any attack would be detected there. Moreover, he clearly did not want his father to know of his plan; so he had to sneak off in the direction of Geba, and from there to cross the ravine.

While Jonathan proceeded to execute his plan, his father remained at Migron at the northern extremity of the territory of Gibeah. Thus he was in a good position to move quickly along the main road to Micmash when pursuit of the Philistines required it. With Saul was Ahijah, the high priest and a great-grandson of Eli, mentioned here (14:3) because of his place in the narrative in verses 18–19, 36–46.

As Jonathan prepared to move against the Philistines, he did not appear as foolhardy but as a courageous man of faith whose confidence was in the power of God. Jonathan seemed to be an instrument in the hand of God for the accomplishment of His purposes. "Uncircumcised" (14:6) is an epithet of derision; but more than that, it classified the Philistines as outside the covenant of God and thus not entitled to His special protection and enablement. As Jonathan launched his venture, he was ably assisted by his brave and ready armorbearer.

Jonathan's plan was to cross the valley and reveal himself to the Philistines. Then he devised a test-sign. If they said, "Come up to us," Jonathan would know that "the LORD has given them into our hands" (14:10). How he came to this conclusion is hard to say, but it may be argued that God had put the thought into his head. It was as much a part of His sovereign plan on this occasion as the servant's formulation of a test when he went to get a bride for Isaac (Gen. 24:12–27). And it was not presumption on Jonathan's part to expect God to make His will clear, for he believed he was engaged in a God-honoring cause.

Commentators often reach the conclusion that the reply "Come up to us," rather than "Wait until we come to you," reflected cowardice on the part of the Philistines. But that is not necessarily true. Perhaps it was more a sign of caution or a desire to avoid unnecessary exposure. They would have a greater position of strength if they fought in their fortified area. Also, the invitation to come up involved a certain amount of ridicule, implying, "Come up if you can, it is really impossible for you to do so." From an Israelite point of view, the invitation to come up reflected a degree of overconfidence and perhaps carelessness on the part of the defenders. Moreover, it gave the Israelites the advantage of a surprise element, for the time and the possibility of their arrival were uncertain. And it gave them cover of foliage and led to the Philistine belief that more attackers were in the bushes. "Wait until we come to you" would indicate a greater degree of aggressive determination and fierceness of fighting spirit.

When Jonathan and his armorbearer made themselves known to the Philistines, the invitation was issued to "come up" (14:12). The two Hebrews went forth in confidence. The precipitous climb was achieved only with considerable effort. When the pair broke into the outpost, the rout was complete. It is not clear what happened. Perhaps the defenders were caught off guard and were without their weapons for the moment; perhaps

there was a divinely imposed disorientation. At any rate Jonathan killed
and wounded many; his armorbearer "put some to death behind him"
(14:13 NASB). It was an armorbearer's duty to kill those his master had
wounded. The pair killed about twenty men, but the last half of verse 14 is
unclear; apparently it indicates a small area, an acre or less. It has been
suggested that apparently a supernatural power similar to that which
felled Jesus' opponents in the Garden of Gethsemane (John 18:6) was
operative here. The panic at the outpost rapidly gripped the entire army.
This was compounded by a severe earthquake. The sacred historian adds,
"It was a panic sent from God" (14:15; literally, "a terror of God").

2. Rout of the Philistines (14:16–23)

Saul's spies or scouts in the vicinity of Gibeah detected a great confusion in the Philistine camp: "the multitude was surging to and fro in all
directions" (14:16). Guessing that some of his men had launched an attack, Saul called for a mustering or parade of the troops to see who was
missing. Of course, Jonathan and his armorbearer were not to be found.
As a reverent and responsible leader of Israel, Saul then sought to learn
from God what course of action his forces should take. The means by
which he sought to make inquiry is not clear. The Hebrew text says Saul
gave a command to bring the "ark of God" (14:18); but the ark had been at
Kiriath Jearim for some time, and there is no reference to its having been
moved from its resting place. Though the ark temporarily may have been
transported to Gibeah, the Septuagint gives a plausible alternate reading:
Abijah the priest was instructed to "bring the ephod," the high priest's
shoulder vestment to which was attached the oracle pouch containing the
Urim and Thummim.

But Saul did not get as far as finding out God's will by this means. The
din in the Philistine camp increased. Evidently divine intervention had
occurred already and immediate action was required. The priest had
stretched out his hand to take the sacred lot but was told, "Withdraw your
hand" (14:19). Saul gave the order to advance. As the men did so they
found the enemy camp in total confusion, with Philistine striking Philistine. When Saul and his men appeared, the Hebrews serving in the
Philistine army, either as mercenaries or conscripts, now had a rallying
point and turned against their masters. Ultimately, the bedlam reached
such a pitch that terrified Israelites who had hidden from the Philistines
emerged from their shelters and pursued the enemy. The rout was complete. God was given the primary credit: "Yahweh rescued Israel that
day" (14:23).

3. Saul's taboo and Jonathan's violation (14:24–35)

It is somewhat unclear as to exactly what is involved in this passage, but
perhaps the following is a reasonable approximation. Without doubt, near

the beginning of the battle, Saul put his men under oath to eat nothing until sundown. This taboo of fasting was presumably regarded as a means of placating God or securing His favor on the endeavor being undertaken. Additionally, Saul may have had in mind the necessity of giving God the first claim to what was captured, but in the oath nothing was said about a prohibition against plunder. Also, it has been alleged that Saul had a false zeal and that in a moment of despotic fervor he had forced his will on his men. It is possible he also had an idea that if his men took time out to eat, they would lose the advantage.

As a result of being bound under oath not to eat, the Israelites were "hard-pressed" or "greatly fatigued" or "driven to exhaustion" (14:24 NEB). When the troops entered the woods, their mouths watered as they saw a generous supply of wild honey "oozing out" (14:26 NIV) of well-filled honeycombs; but they did not break their oath. Jonathan, not knowing about the oath, dipped his staff in the honey as he went by and ate some. Very soon "his eyes brightened" (v. 27), i.e., they lost the dull, glazed look of exhaustion and returned to their normal luster. Then one of the soldiers told Jonathan about the oath and the curse Saul had laid on the troops. Jonathan then spoke critically of his father, saying that he "has troubled the land" (14:29), i.e., has made it impossible to take full advantage of the victory because the Israelite army was exhausted.

All that day the Israelites pursued and fought the Philistines, from Micmash westward to Aijalon, a distance of well over fifteen miles. They were totally exhausted. And when the sun set at last, they voraciously pounced on captured sheep and cattle and slew them on the ground in such a way that there was no proper drainage of the blood from the animals, as required under the Mosaic Law (Lev. 19:26; Deut. 12:16). When Saul learned of this breach of the law, he appointed a large stone as a place of slaughtering so the blood could be properly separated from the animals. Then Saul built an altar in that place, probably not for sacrifice, but as a memorial of God's presence with them and His power on their behalf.

4. *Jonathan's guilt and rescue* (14:36–46)

After what must have been a lengthy period of rest and refreshment, Saul proposed that the Israelites pursue the Philistines and destroy them utterly. Perhaps his mention of "spoil" (14:36) was meant as an inducement to weary men to fight on. The army seemed willing but Ahijah, the priest, recommended that they seek the will of God in the matter. When God did not respond at all (through the Urim and Thummim of the high priest), Saul concluded that some sin in their midst had caused God to turn away from them. In order to discover the source of the trouble, Saul directed that they cast lots. He put the army chiefs in one group and himself and Jonathan in another, declaring under oath that if Jonathan were guilty, he would die. The lot fell on Saul and Jonathan, and the people went free; a second lot fell on Jonathan.

Jonathan confessed his fault; and in conformity to his vow before God, Saul condemned him to death. Nothing is said about Jonathan's pleading ignorance; presumably the point was made. The people underscored the fact that God had saved Israel through Jonathan that day and refused to let harm befall him. What is involved here is as difficult to discover and explain as was the meaning of 1 Samuel 14:24–35. Apparently what Jonathan did was not wrong in itself, but it became wrong because of Saul's oath. And as Keil and Delitzsch have observed, "The breach of a command issued with a solemn oath, even when it took place unconsciously, excited the wrath of God, as being a profanation of the divine name" (p. 147). When the lot fell on Jonathan, God was not pronouncing the death sentence. Rather, God was showing that Jonathan had violated his father's oath that was made in God's name. Evidently both Saul's vow prohibiting eating until sundown and the one committing him to judgment of death on Jonathan were very rash. However one evaluates all this, Saul did not get any marching orders from God; so he decided to return home. For their part, the Philistines withdrew from Israelite territory in the hills of Samaria and restricted their activities to the Mediterranean coastland.

5. *General summary of Saul's family and his wars* (14:47–52)

So much emphasis is placed on Saul's personal failures in Scripture and in the minds of Bible students that often his military successes are overlooked. His victories were almost as extensive as those of David, though his conquests were not so permanent as those of his successor. East of the Jordan he defeated the Edomites on the south, and then the Moabites and Ammonites, conquering all the way up to Zobah, north of Damascus (v. 47). But though he fought "bitter warfare" (14:52) with the Philistines on the west all during the rest of his reign, he never subdued them. The members of his family are named in verse 49, and the commander of his forces was his cousin Abner. It is known that he had an additional son, Ish-Bosheth (2 Sam. 2:8; cf. 1 Chron. 8:33; 9:39).

F. Saul's Disobedience and Rejection (15:1–35)

Saul's first major test had come at Gilgal near the beginning of his reign. Failure, as demonstrated by lack of faith and intrusion into the priestly office, had brought the divine pronouncement that his dynasty would extend only through his own reign (13:13–14). Now God comes to Saul with a second test. Perhaps there is a hint that he is being given a second chance to make good, though that is not specifically stated. Unfortunately, he did not make good; his partial obedience resulted in God's rejection of his kingship (v. 26). Thereafter he increasingly lost his grip on his kingdom and even on his sanity.

To establish his right to deliver God's command to Saul, Samuel reminded the king that he had been God's agent for putting him in office. In essence, the command was to obliterate the Amalekites. Literally, the order was "to devote," or irrevocably give over, the Amalekites and all that belonged to them to Yahweh. The means of accomplishing such a feat in this case and in many others was by total destruction as an act of God's judgment (cf. Deut. 7:2; 20:17). The basis for God's judgment was Amalekite treatment of the Israelites at the time of the Exodus (Exod. 17:8–16; cf. Deut. 25:17–19). But there was more to Amalekite harassment of Israel than the one event in history. They had opposed Israel's entrance to Canaan (Num. 14:25) and were implacable enemies during the period of the judges (cf. Judg. 3:13; 6:3). Finally, their quota of iniquity seems to have been reached, as evidently occurred with other peoples from time to time (cf. Gen. 15:16; Deut. 20:17). Then God ordered their destruction. The Amalekites were descendants of Esau (Gen. 36:12), who lived south of Judah in the area between Beersheba and the Sinai.

The promptness with which Saul mobilized the troops gave promise of the faithful execution of the divine orders. The place of mustering the troops, Telaim, cannot be identified (15:4). The number of Israelites called up is not unduly large, considering the nature of the operation. The Amalekites lived in a seminomadic state, and it would have required numerous contingents of troops to chase them over the countryside. In fact, Saul attacked them "all the way from Havilah to Shur, to the east of Egypt" (15:7 NIV), from northwest Arabia to the eastern border of Egypt, i.e., the line of the Suez Canal. Saul himself concentrated on "the city of Amalek" (15:5), perhaps the only settled population center among them. What and where it was are unknown. As he prepared to ambush the city, he advised the Kenites to flee so they would not be destroyed too. The Kenites, old allies of Israel, were the tribe of Moses' father-in-law (Judg. 1:16; 4:11; Num. 10:29). The historian now spells out Saul's incomplete obedience. Saul and his army spared King Agag, the best of the livestock, and other attractive booty. Everyone else and everything else was destroyed.

At that point God told Samuel about Saul's incomplete obedience. In saying "I repent" (15:11; "regret") having made Saul king, God was not indicating a changeableness in His nature. From a divine standpoint, God is steadfast and unchangeable. His holiness and justice require that sin be dealt with. But often in Scripture His promises and threats are presented as conditional. That is, blessing attends reverence for God, but punishment follows disobedience. In this particular case God had insisted that Hebrew kings be God-fearing; and Saul was warned that if he failed to honor God, divine anointing would be abrogated; he would be rejected.

Now that Saul had failed God at least twice, God had to deal with this incapacity. Thus divine "repentance," or change of mind, toward Saul was consistent with His unchangeable character. And once God had determined a course of action and announced a judgment, no alteration was to be expected. Human pleas could not change God's mind (cf. 15:29). So from God's standpoint, He is truly unchangeable; but from a human standpoint, He may appear to change. And sometimes, to accommodate Himself to human understanding, He may even lead the inspired writers of Scripture to speak of God's changing His mind.

The details of God's conversation with Samuel are not related here; they come out in the subsequent exchange between Samuel and Saul. Samuel was deeply distressed over this judgment; in fact, the prophet expressed some anger or indignation over the whole matter. No doubt he was disturbed because if the king were deposed, his own authority and confidence would be eroded, the nation would suffer confusion, and God would be subjected to blasphemy and abuse at the hands of confused and doubting Israelites.

After a sleepless night Samuel went out to find Saul. He learned that the king had gone to Carmel, not Mount Carmel but a town in Judah about ten miles southeast of Hebron (15:12). There he had erected some sort of monument to himself, probably a victory memorial, and then he had gone to Gilgal. At the latter place the prophet caught up with him.

When Samuel arrived Saul extended a cheerful and friendly welcome, presumably as a bold hypocrite, and claimed to have fulfilled God's orders. His subsequent statements indicate that he knew he had disobeyed God. Samuel unmasked him immediately with an inquiry about all the livestock around the camp. Saul first sought to shift the blame, a tack as old as the Garden of Eden (Gen. 3; cf. Exod. 32:22). In taking this approach Saul solved nothing because he was, after all, commander-in-chief and should have been able to enforce his will; he was able to do so the day of the battle recounted in the previous chapter. If he truly was manipulated by his men to disobey God, he was not fit to be God's anointed king. Thus if he was right, if he was a tool of the people, he was in trouble with both men and God; the situation was out of control. Then Saul went on to say that the best Amalekite animals had been saved for sacrifice to God. That sounded good, but all the animals were supposed to be "devoted" to God. In killing the worst ones, they had given God only the undesirable ones. The ones saved for sacrifice would not really go to God anyway because in the peace offerings nearly all of the animal was consumed by the worshipers in a communal meal.

As Saul proceeded to justify himself, Samuel broke in, saying, "Stop!" (15:16 NIV), or "Leave off" excusing yourself any further. "When you were little in your own eyes" (15:17; cf. 9:21), God made you king over Israel and sent you on a mission to exterminate the Amalekites. Why did you disobey God? Why have you arrogantly set aside God's instructions?

Saul still wanted to justify himself. He argued that he had obeyed God, that he had exterminated the Amalekites; all that was left was their king, and the soldiers did well in saving animals for sacrifice. The best of the booty had been saved for God, the giver of victory, a praiseworthy sign of piety (Num. 31:48). But what was "devoted" to God belonged to Him already, as noted above, and could not be offered to Him as a sacrifice (Lev. 27:29; Deut. 13:16). In passing, it is interesting to note that in verses 15 and 21 Saul refers to "the LORD your God" in speaking to Samuel. One wonders how much He was Saul's God too.

Samuel chose not to debate the question of whether animals under the ban could be used for sacrifice and returned to the issue of obedience. Saul had been commanded to exterminate the Amalekites and to destroy all their belongings, not to come back with sacrifices. Samuel did not condemn sacrifices but asserted that to obey was better than sacrifice. After all, sacrifices were an expression of faith and piety. Whenever the external observance was considered to be more important than inner spiritual health, one's religion was askew. Further emphasizing the importance of agreement between the externals of religion and the faith of the heart, Samuel observed that disobedience or rebellion was as bad as the practice of witchcraft, and arrogance or presumption as bad as the practice of idolatry. Conscious disobedience is like idolatry in that it sets up the human will in place of God. Then he pronounced the terrible sentence: "Because you have rejected the word of the LORD, he has also rejected you from being king" (15:26).

That broke Saul. His pretenses were gone. "I have sinned" (15:30), he cried. But from what follows, it is frequently argued that his confession was not genuine. In support of such a view is his continued effort to put the blame on his soldiers and his desire for the presence of Samuel to prevent loss of control over the kingdom. In reply, it is in order to warn against judging the sincerity of another's confession to God and the nature and validity of the motives for making the confession. In this case Saul honestly may have been confessing with great heartbreak that he had allowed himself to be misled by the cupidity of his men. Moreover, he honestly may have wanted forgiveness and the company of Samuel with the divine sustenance that the presence of the prophet meant to him.

Samuel refused to return with Saul, both because Saul had rejected the dictates of God and because God had therefore rejected his rule over Israel. It is significant, however, that Samuel did not refuse forgiveness; nor does the text say that God refused forgiveness. God may forgive one's sin, but that does not mean He eliminates the effects of it. God will forgive the embezzler, but the criminal act will stain his reputation to his dying day. God will forgive a murderer, but He will not bring the victim back to life. God could forgive Saul, but He would not give him back the kingdom on the same basis that he had it before. Then as Samuel turned to leave, Saul in desperation grabbed hold of the prophet's outer robe and tore it off him (15:27). Samuel used this accident as a further symbolic judgment on Saul: just so "Yahweh has torn the sovereignty of Israel from you today" (15:28; cf. 1 Kings 11:29–31).

When Saul renewed his plea for Samuel to return to Gibeah to lend his support to the monarchy, Samuel agreed this time. In so doing, he could help preserve outward order in Israel until a new king was anointed; and he could carry out the ban on Agag. The manner in which Agag appeared before Samuel is not clear from the Hebrew text. Some conclude that he came "cheerfully" (15:32; confidently," NIV), feeling that the immediate danger of death was past; and others, "fearfully" or "haltingly," because he was in fetters and thought that death was imminent. In any case Samuel was determined to execute the ban against Agag. Or his execution could be viewed as capital punishment because evidently he had fought his wars with great cruelty. Probably aged Samuel did not kill Agag personally but ordered some soldier to do it. "Before the LORD" (15:33) means before the altar at Gilgal.

After the events at Gilgal, Samuel left for his home at Ramah, and Saul went to his home at Gibeah. The relationship between the two was irretrievably broken. The usual translation of verse 35 is that "Samuel did not see Saul again until the day of his death" (RSV). But perhaps the better rendering is that Samuel "did not go to see Saul again" (NIV) because the two presumably did meet one more time when Saul pursued David (1 Sam. 19:24). However, they may not have conversed on that occasion; and it is possible that "before Samuel" (1 Sam. 19:24) meant only near him and not actually in his sight. "Samuel mourned for Saul" (15:35 KJV), lamented all his days for this once great man.

For Further Study

1. What good and bad qualities of Saul are revealed in 1 Samuel 8–15?

2. In Samuel's farewell address (1 Sam. 12), he was cleared of any wrongdoing. Did he exemplify any inadequacies?

3. Write a paragraph summary of the kind of person God expected a king of Israel to be.

4. Make a list of reasons why Israel wanted a king.

5. Make a list of leadership functions that Samuel performed in 1 Samuel 8–15.

Chapter 3

The Decline of Saul and the Rise of David (I)
From David's Anointing to His Flight
(1 Samuel 16:1–20:42)

God's rejection of Saul was a private action. Presumably no one knew of it except the prophet and the king. The government continued to function as it had for some time. How Samuel explained his absence from the court is not known, but he must have been able to deal with the question in some evasive way. In the minds of God and of Samuel, Saul was no longer a theocratic ruler; and the kingdom was therefore shepherdless in the truest sense of the term. It was unthinkable that God would leave the nation in such a state of affairs indefinitely. He finally instructed Samuel to stop his grieving for the rejected sovereign and exercise his powers as kingmaker once more.

A. David's Anointing and Introduction to the Court (16:1–23)

The instruction was specific enough: go to Bethlehem and anoint one of the sons of Jesse as king. Samuel's reticence is not to be interpreted merely as fear for his personal safety. To anoint or attempt to anoint another king would be viewed as an act of treason and worthy of death for himself and the king-designate. Moreover, there was the question of how he would be received in Bethlehem; and there was the possibility of a civil war following the anointing. No doubt most of this was in Samuel's mind when he asked, "How can I go?" (16:2).

God did not rebuke Samuel for his fear but gave him a workable plan for accomplishing his task. He was to take a calf for a sacrifice, to call Jesse and his sons to the sacrifice, and to anoint one of them king. "I will show you what to do" (16:3 NIV) is a tremendous statement of assurance for any believer sent on a mission. It is not necessary to have a blueprint or roadmap showing all the details in advance. "The steps of a good man are ordered by the LORD" (Ps. 37:23 KJV), and he may trust God for all the details along the way.

So Samuel went to Bethlehem, more than twenty-five miles south of Ramah. His arrival sent the populace into paroxysms of fear: "the elders

. . . came trembling to meet him" (16:4). The town was far south of Samuel's usual judicial circuit, and they concluded that he must have come to perform some special act of judgment. He assured them that he had come in peace and that he intended to offer a sacrifice there; the calf he had brought with him probably was substantial evidence of the truth of what he said. The offering of a sacrifice in various places became an accepted practice because there was no longer a central sanctuary. When the elders took his statements at face value, Samuel then instructed them to "sanctify" (16:5 KJV; "consecrate," NIV; "purify," JB) themselves in preparation for the sacred event. Evidently legal purification preceded any sacrificial festival (cf. Exod. 19:10, 22). Samuel gave special attention to the purification of Jesse's sons.

There were three stages to this sacred festival: the consecration, the sacrifice, and the sacrificial or fellowship meal that followed. The details of the proceedings are passed over in silence, with attention being focused on the main purpose for the sacrifice: the anointing of a new king. It is not at all clear when the anointing took place. The usual view is that it occurred during a private sacrificial or fellowship meal for Jesse's family, but it seems to make some sense to place it during the consecration ceremony. At that time Samuel could and did examine each of the sons individually, and the anointing would have aroused less suspicion then.

At any rate Samuel did evaluate each of Jesse's sons with a view to kingship. Certainly, Jesse knew that something of a process of choice was going on; but the kingship was never mentioned to him or to David later on. The sons seem not to have been told anything of the purpose of the gathering. As the sons passed in review, Samuel was impressed with the eldest, no doubt in part because of the law of primogeniture and in part because of his size and handsome physique. God made it very clear to the prophet that one can be misled very easily by outward appearances; God is concerned with inner qualities. How much of the conversation in verses 6–9 was audible or addressed to Jesse is not clear. Surely verse 6 records what Samuel thought and verse 7 what God said to him. The statements of rejection in verses 8–9 may have been addressed to Jesse, and certainly the declaration in verse 10 was.

After seven sons had passed in review, it would appear that either a mistake had been made or there were more sons somewhere. Jesse admitted that there was a young son out tending the sheep. Samuel's statement that they would not sit down (i.e., to eat the sacrificial meal) until he was brought in is usually thought to indicate that this review took place during the sacrificial meal. But if David was at some distance, and if someone else had to be found to watch the sheep, a time lapse was required that could have been provided by the sacrifice and preparation of the meal.

Of course, it must be admitted that it is not necessary to put the review during the purification process; the sons could have passed before the aged prophet for his special blessing while the calf was roasting and the group was waiting to eat. In any event David finally arrived and made a pleasing appearance. But his choice had to be on bases other than that, as verse 7 makes clear. In order to support an emphasis on inner qualities, the Septuagint inserts in verse 12 the words "goodly in the sight of the Lord" to characterize David. David is described as "ruddy" (16:12; probably with auburn hair and fair complexion instead of the usual black hair and dark complexion), "with beautiful eyes" (v. 12), and "handsome features" (v. 12 NIV; graceful and well proportioned). God instructed Samuel to anoint David; and he did so immediately "in the midst of his brothers" (v. 13). What they thought is not indicated. They could have concluded that Samuel was choosing his successor and need not have been unduly suspicious.

Though the brothers were not informed of the significance of what was going on, probably David and possibly even Jesse were given at least an inkling of the truth. David's return to his flock of sheep was quite natural. He was in no position to do anything else until God told him what to do and cleared the way for him to do it. Taking up his old occupation was no necessary indication that he did not know the purpose of the anointing.

From the moment of the anointing, the Holy Spirit came upon David to train him for his great work and to give him the courage and wisdom to be a truly great king of Israel. That enduement evidently did not result in any ecstatic experience, for none is recorded. The Holy Spirit likewise had come upon Saul after his anointing (1 Sam. 10:6) and had provided enablement for him during the years of his kingship. But now that Saul's disobedience had brought God's complete rejection and a new king was being groomed for the job, that Spirit of enablement left Saul (16:14). It should be added that the ministry of the Holy Spirit in the lives of either Old or New Testament saints does not guarantee infallibility in their thought processes or victory in all the circumstances of life.

As the power of the Holy Spirit left Saul,[1] he no longer had the resources to enable him to run the kingdom, or even to maintain his mental health. In fact, as a punishment God sent on him a form of severe depression. As time went on it became more severe and perhaps was not far removed from a psychotic condition. Certainly, Saul's state was aggravated by brooding over rejection by God and his sense of inadequacy as a ruler. The only treatment Saul's attendants knew for such a malady was the soothing music of a harp. Or perhaps it is better to call it a lyre, for it

[1]A distinction must be drawn between the ministry of the Holy Spirit in the Old Testament and the New. In the Old Testament, He came upon individuals to empower them to do specific tasks. For example, He gave Bezaleel the craftsmanship to build the tabernacle (Exod. 31:1–5), and He gave Saul and David qualities necessary to rule Israel. Believers today are indwelt by the Holy Spirit when they believe, and they retain His presence throughout their lives (cf. 1 Cor. 6:19; Rom. 8:9–15).

was a small stringed instrument in the form of a flat-sounding box with two wooden arms joined by a crosspiece. The strings were stretched from the box to the crosspiece. Saul listened to his advisers and instructed them to find an accomplished musician.

One of the courtiers knew about David in Bethlehem, only about nine miles from Gibeah. David seemed eminently qualified. He was an excellent musician, a brave man, and a fighter who had killed lions and bears (1 Sam. 17:34–35). He also was skilled in the use of words, was handsome, and was blessed of God. Saul was impressed and fired off a request to Jesse for the services of his son. Whatever Jesse may have thought about the demand, he had no alternative but to comply. He sent along as a token of homage a donkey loaded with bread, a skin of wine, and a young goat. The gifts show the simplicity of the customs of Israel and the court of Saul at the time.

Saul was very much impressed with David and even made him his armorbearer. In fact, he communicated his good pleasure to Jesse and requested David's continued services. In the early stages of Saul's psychological difficulties, whenever he was plagued with one of his fits of despondency, David was able to restore him to normalcy with his music (16:23). Later this did not work, as the scene in 1 Samuel 19:9–10 demonstrates.

Curiosity as to the nature of Saul's palace at Gibeah has been satisfied by excavations at the site. The palace-fortress was a rectangular structure that measured 169 by 114 feet and had towers extending from each of the four corners.

B. David's Contest With Goliath (17:1–58)

Evidently David did not always remain at the court but was temporarily on loan from his family. His services were probably not needed on a regular basis (cf. 17:15). While he was back in Bethlehem, the Philistines moved up the Valley of Elah on one of their periodic incursions into the territory of Israel. They advanced as far as Socoh, about fourteen miles west of Bethlehem, and camped at Ephes Dammim, about a mile northwest of Socoh. Of course, the Israelites had mustered to meet the threat, and the two armies stood facing each other on the hills that rose on either side of the Valley of Elah.

At length a champion came down from the Philistine side of the valley and strode into the valley itself to taunt the Israelites. He proposed that single combat replace fighting between the two armies. Such a procedure is known from both Semitic and Greek sources (e.g., the combat between Achilles and Hector recorded in Book 7 of The Iliad). The fight between twelve men from each side in 2 Samuel 2:12–16 is only a variation of the principle.

This champion could afford to make the offer of 17:9 because he was reasonably confident no one in the Israelite camp could match him. He was probably not without parallel among the Philistines, however. The tall Anakim, though no longer existing in Israel after Joshua's day, continued to live in Gaza, Gath, and Ashdod (Josh. 11:22). From Gath, Goliath was fearsome indeed. He stood to a height of six cubits and a span. If the cubit is computed at the commonly accepted length of seventeen and one-half inches and the span at about nine inches, the height of the giant was about nine feet six inches. His body was protected by a coat of chain mail made of bronze (giving the appearance of overlapping scales of fish) and weighing about one hundred twenty-five pounds. He had a bronze helmet and bronze greaves or shin guards and had a javelin slung across his back. The wooden shaft of his spear was as big as a weaver's beam (a pole or beam from a large loom), and it had an iron point weighing about fifteen pounds. Of course, he had a sword at his side; and before this formidable warrior, well protected by body armor, walked a shield bearer. Goliath terrified the armies of Israel, not only with his appearance, but also with his braggadocio. His taunts were heard every morning and evening as he challenged the Israelites (17:16). "Forty days" is taken by some to be a general statement, indicating a long period of time. Otherwise, if literal, it may be variously interpreted. It was possibly the total period of time he did this before David struck him down.

Though it is not clear why the historical information in 17:12–15 is presented as if David had not been introduced earlier, the facts given are necessary to the account. David's three oldest brothers were at the front, and Jesse wanted to find out how they were and to send them a "care package." Actually, there was no central commissariat, and the men in the army were dependent on supplies from home. Jesse sent an ephah (about a half bushel) of parched grain (wheat or barley roasted when it was ripe) and ten loaves or cakes (shaped like pancakes) of bread for his sons and ten small soft cheeses for their commander.

Obeying his father's wishes, David left early the next morning and arrived in camp just as the army was going into battle positions; they shouted the war cry as they took their stations. The Philistines were going through the same motions. David left his supplies with a member of the quartermaster corps and ran to the battle lines to find his brothers. As he stood talking with them and as the two armies glowered at each other across the narrow valley, Goliath came forth as before to shout his challenge to the Israelites. And he struck the same fear into the hearts of his opponents as before.

In talking with the men in their stations along the crest of the hill, David heard a report about a reward to be given to the one who killed Goliath: riches, the king's daughter in marriage, and freedom from various kinds of public obligations. David grew increasingly interested in this reward and evidently went to several to ask about it. The answer was similar in each case, and it is possible that David let some hints drop in connection with these inquiries that he would be interested in fighting Goliath. At this distance in time and place from the event, and hampered by a very brief summary in Scripture, it is hard for us to know David's motives for wanting to get involved. Perhaps he was looking for a road to riches and glory, or possibly the situation called forth his courageous spirit, or maybe he had sufficient understanding of his anointing to believe he would live through this challenge to become the king, or he may have wanted to vindicate the name and reputation of God before these pagans (see especially 17:26). And who can prove that the Spirit of God was not prompting him to take on this pagan, who not only threw taunts against the Israelites but also against their God?

In the midst of David's conversations at the front, his eldest brother, Eliab, overheard him and angrily rebuked him. He clearly spoke out of jealousy of his younger brother, and what he said seems to reflect a deeply rooted jealousy rather than an irritation of the moment. The accusation is interpreted to mean that David was not content with his lowly calling but had proud and ambitious aspirations; he was not interested in seeing his brothers but wanted to see the battle. It may be that he had wanted to go to war himself and was refused and/or had talked at home of his desire to help rid Israel of her Philistine oppressors.

David's reply in 17:29 is hard to interpret. It may mean, as the NASB and RSV indicate, "What is wrong with what I have done? I was just asking a question." Or the last half of 17:29, following the KJV, may be taken to mean, "Isn't what I have said justified? Can't it be expected that God will help some Israelite to beat this insufferable pagan?"

In any event David continued to talk to various men at their posts. In the process he indicated an interest in fighting Goliath. Finally his conversations were reported to Saul, who had been eagerly looking for a champion. When Saul sent for him, David volunteered to fight the Philistine. Saul argued that Goliath was a seasoned warrior, while David was a youth untrained in warfare. David responded with impressive credentials of his own. He had had extensive and successful combat experience with lions and bears while protecting his father's sheep. The tense in the original is imperfect and indicates repetitive action. Thus one should not conclude that David tackled only one bear and one lion. Verse 34 might better be translated, "Whenever a lion or a bear" (JB). Not only did David have combat experience and an abundance of courage reflected in it, but he also had abundant faith in God to deliver him from the Philistine. This faith met with a like response from Saul, who said, "Go then . . . and the LORD will be with you" (17:37 NEB).

Saul then proceeded to prepare David for the contest. First he dressed him in his own tunic and coat of mail, perhaps a hint that David one day would take Saul's place as king. That it was possible for David to wear

Saul's clothes indicates both the loosefitting nature of the garments and the substantial size of David. The unusual size of Saul has been noted, but there is not reason to conclude that David was a stripling; he was merely the youngest son of his father. Goliath's ridicule of David's size was part of his psychological warfare, and anyone in the Israelite camp would have been small compared to him. It is not clear whether the bronze helmet and the other armor that Saul provided for David were his own. Nor is it clear whose sword was involved in 17:39; the Hebrew text intimates it was David's.

After David was completely outfitted, he began to walk around in all that weight. The equipment was strange to him; he had not "tested" (17:39 NASB; "proved," KJV) it, i.e., he had no experiential acquaintance with it. He found it to be an impediment instead of a help; so he took it off. David's effectiveness lay in ease and rapidity of movement. He would have made a terrible mistake if he had tried to fight Goliath on the latter's terms. Sometimes Christian workers make the mistake David avoided: they try to do the work of God or fight the enemies of God with techniques someone else prescribes instead of seeking means suited or individualized to their own personalities and training.

David took his shepherd's staff and sling. The former was not much of a weapon against Goliath. It could be used as a walking stick to help him get down the side of the ravine into the valley, and no doubt it had been used to club wild animals. The sling was a deadly weapon, however. Made of two ropes attached to a thong of leather or goat hair into which a stone could be fitted, it could hurl a stone a considerable distance with hair's breadth accuracy. Benjamites from the area of Gibeah were especially known for their prowess as slingers (Judg. 20:14–16). Other Israelites were accomplished in the use of slings too, and slingers were a regular part of the army. Assyrians also had contingents of slingers, as their monuments attest. Anyone who has seen modern Arab boys using their slings knows how terrifying and deadly they can be. In preparation for battle, David chose five smooth stones from the wadi or dry stream bed at the edge of the Valley of Elah and put them in his shepherd's bag.

Then the two combatants began to advance against each other. As Goliath sized up David, he saw that he was a young man—not a seasoned warrior—and began his psychological warfare. He taunted David and cursed him "by his gods" (17:43). It is clear from David's response that this cursing involved defiance not only against David but also against the God of Israel. Such braggadocio was always dangerous for the pagan enemies of Israel. They fancied that Yahweh was no more powerful than the gods they served. But in such cases God was bound to demonstrate His power, for His name's sake. To Goliath's ridicule, David responded with some psychological warfare of his own. He showed that he had some ability with words (cf. 16:18), but what he said was not merely empty verbal abuse. It was a kind of manifesto of the power of Yahweh about to descend on one who dared to defy Him, on one who supposed he could stand against the devastating might of Israel's God. And "the whole world" (17:46; Gentiles present and many who will hear of this event) and "those gathered here" (17:47), or "this congregation"; a term for the assembly of Israel) will see an apologetic for the existence and power of God acted out before their eyes. God is not dependent on heavy armor for victory in battle.

As the two closed in on each other, David utilized speed and surprise. One well-aimed stone to the forehead of the Philistine downed him. Since the rest of his body was well protected with armor, why aim there? It is not clear whether the stone killed Goliath or merely knocked him out, with death coming by decapitation. Nor, in the Hebrew text, is it clear whether David used his own sword or Goliath's to behead the giant. But the effect was the same.

According to the terms of the challenge, the Philistines now should have submitted to the Israelites, but they fled in fear. The Israelites followed in hot pursuit all the way to the Philistine cities of Gath, about seven miles west, and Ekron, about the same distance to the northwest. Fleeing men are no match for attackers, and the carnage among the Philistines was heavy. The Israelites, having no resources for a siege of the Philistine cities, circled back to their own camp and plundered the Philistine camp on the way.

David's taking the head of Goliath to Jerusalem has led the critics to express considerable doubt as to the accuracy of the text, for he did not conquer Jerusalem and make it the capital of united Israel until some years later (2 Sam. 5). But it should be noted that Israelites took up residence there at the time of the conquest (Josh. 15:63) and wrought considerable damage on the Canaanite city during the period of the judges (Judg. 1:8). They were not able to conquer the Canaanite citadel until much later, however. We can presume then, for a long time Hebrews and Jebusites lived side by side in two parts of Jerusalem, much as Jews and Arabs did before the Six Day War in 1967. David probably took Goliath's armor to his own tent or his home thereafter, but later Goliath's sword appeared at the sanctuary at Nob (1 Sam. 21:9). It was possibly given as a kind of votive offering to God.

The chapter concludes with a curious investigation into David's identity (17:55–58). It is common for critics to question it, dismiss it, or locate it elsewhere because it seems inexplicable here and because the Septuagint does not include it. But it is not necessary to reject this account as spurious. In the first place, Abner easily could have been ignorant of David by name. He may have been absent from court whenever David was present to wait on Saul. Second, David may have matured considerably during his absence from the court; and now, with a full beard, he was virtually unrecognizable. Third, David may not have been very close to the disturbed king when he played for him, and the tiny oil lamps of the day did not provide enough light to illuminate the features of a person at a distance. Moreover, if Saul were in a truly disturbed state, he may not have paid any attention to those around him nor have cared about who they were. In fact, he may have kept his eyes closed and have reclined while David played for him. Now, in a full Palestinian sun, a beared young man was fully and perceptibly visible to a king who was temporarily enjoying a high level of mental and emotional health; and he inquired about the liberator of Israel.

C. David's Flight From Saul's Jealousy (18:1–20:42)

1. *David's acceptance by the royal family* (18:1–5)

As David finished talking with Saul after the destruction of Goliath, Jonathan's heart was strangely warmed toward David: "The soul of Jonathan "bound itself [literally 'chained itself'] to David's soul" (18:1). Presumably the basis for this deep love on the part of Jonathan was twofold: the beautiful qualities he saw in David and the Lord's presence with him. David reciprocated that love, and the bond was strengthened by the fact that both of them were engaged in the same struggle against the enemies of God. Then they formalized their love relationship in a solemn covenant, and Jonathan ratified it with the bestowal of clothing and weapons on David. In a sense this giving away of clothing amounted to a giving away of one's own self. Although the exchange of clothing in connection with making a covenant is known among various ancient peoples, in this case it symbolized or prefigured Jonathan's forfeiture of the kingship to David. If Jonathan did not recognize the inevitability of this transfer of royalty at the time, he did later (cf. 20:12–15). This covenant was kept until Jonathan's death and by David after that. They were truly "brothers" and their love for each other was "more wonderful than that of women" (2 Sam. 1:26).

It was a beautiful relationship. But our sordid generation perverts everything it touches; it cannot seem to take such friendships at face value. It cannot seem to accept the idea that two men could be true, normal friends, united to each other by the love of God and giving themselves to each other unselfishly, without ulterior motives and without asking, "What's in it for me?" Many in recent years have viewed this love covenant as a homosexual pact. But there is no evidence to support such a hypothesis. Both were brave warriors, married, and had children; and David's plurality of wives and lapse with Bathsheba are hardly to be expected of a homosexual.

Not only did Jonathan love and accept David, but Saul also received him into his entourage. From this point on Saul kept David at court constantly and did not permit his periodic extended stays in Bethlehem as before. Moreover, Saul gave David military assignments that he carried out successfully and for which he earned high rank in the army. David evidently carried his success so well and made such a great contribution to the security of the state that the "people" (18:5; primarily the army and the court) and the officers in the army were pleased with his promotions. Verse 5 seems to indicate both an immediate promotion for David and later advancements, for all this achievement could not have occurred before the army returned after the Philistine campaign just described.

2. David's popularity and Saul's jealousy (18:6–30)

No sooner had Saul assigned David to his court than he began to be jealous of him. As the Israelite army wended its way from the front toward Gibeah, it passed numerous villages from which the women poured out to express their joy over the destruction of Goliath and the Philistine forces. They celebrated with a kind of choral dancing, proceeding in long lines and stepping backward and forward and repeating certain verses. They sang antiphonally or responsively and accompanied themselves with tambourines and triangles or three-stringed instruments (perhaps lutelike instruments). Their intent was probably to give the customary honor to the victor; but unfortunately they praised a subject at the expense of his sovereign and thus stirred up anger and jealousy in the heart of the king. Saul's response may have been somewhat exaggerated, but the question at the end of 18:8 is understandable because the adulation was such as would be expressed to a king. "And Saul was looking at David with suspicion from that day on" (18:9).

"The next day" (18:10) could refer to the day after returning to Gibeah from the battle in the Valley of Elah, and the fit of depression he suffered on that day could have been brought on by the adulation of the women in the Israelite towns. But process is hinted at in this chapter (18:5, 9, 13–16, 19), and there may be a gap in the narrative before this "next day" arrived. In any case Saul was experiencing one of his fits of depression. The term "prophesying" in some versions of 18:10 is an unfortunate translation; Saul actually was seized with a violent raving. Of course, David began to play his lyre as at other times, but on this occasion Saul apparently identified David as the source of some of his troubles. The javelin he held in his hand as a scepter now became a weapon for David's destruction. Saul tried twice to kill David but failed to hit him, in part because of his own disorientation in his emotional state, in part because of David's agility, and in part because of the special protection of God.

Verse 12 may be viewed as a conclusion to the attack on David, or it may more properly introduce what follows. Recognizing that God was with David, Saul became increasingly uneasy around him and feared the loss of his throne to him. Therefore he decided to remove him from his sight and from the support of Jonathan and some of the fawning courtiers by sending him into a form of honorable exile: a military appointment at some distance. That move just compounded Saul's problems because now David circulated more widely among the populace; and with his outstanding success in all his tasks (under the blessing of God), he won their hearts. The reference to "Israel and Judah" (18:16) is another reminder that that division existed among the Hebrews from the end of the days of the judges and did not suddenly occur with the division of the kingdom in the days of Rehoboam (1 Kings 12).

Saul's malevolent acts toward David continued throughout the rest of chapter 18. After his direct attack on David's life (18:11), he regained his composure; thereafter he sought to dispose of his rival by indirect means. Perhaps the Philistines would do his dirty work for him. After God's signal blessing on David during the contest with Goliath, Saul should have known better. He used the offer of marriage to his daughter to try to get David killed at the hands of the Philistines. Actually, no further service should have been necessary for the hand of Saul's daughter if the report circulating among the troops at the time of the threats of Goliath was true. The victor was supposed to have this prize as one of his rewards. Now perhaps Saul felt obligated to make good on that offer, especially as David's esteem grew among the people. But he verbalized additional stipulations. One was that David should engage in certain conflicts with the Philistines. Saul's hope was that the Philistines would kill David (18:17). David modestly declared his unworthiness to marry Merab, Saul's daughter. When David did not fall in battle, and presumably because Merab did not want David anyway, Saul found a pretext to marry her to someone else (18:19).

It then became known that Saul's younger daughter, Michal, had fallen in love with David. This gave Saul an opportunity to use her as a "bait" ("snare," 18:21) to lure him to destruction. This time Saul approached David indirectly through his servants, both because it would not be in order for the king to approach David directly on behalf of his daughter and because it may have been difficult for him to do so after the Merab situation. In the negotiations David emphasized the poverty of his family in order to show that he did not have the wherewithal to pay the bride-price or to provide the expected gift to the father of the bride.

Saul countered by saying that he was not really interested in a monetary gift but would like to take vengeance on his enemies. Therefore he asked for one hundred foreskins of the Philistines by a given date. Perhaps the reason for this unusual petition was to put emphasis on the uncircumcised condition of these enemies of the Lord. The fulfillment of the request would, of course, entail the deaths of these Philistines. Whether Saul would have been aware that some other Near Eastern peoples cut off the genitals of enemy soldiers is not known. For example, this practice may be seen on Egyptian monuments. David and his men offered Saul double what he asked, and Saul had no choice but to give David his daughter in marriage.

Now Saul became even more afraid of David, for it was evident that God was with David. The effort to get him killed by the Philistines had not worked, and David was his son-in-law with some possible claim to the throne on that basis. Moreover, as the Philistines made periodic incursions into Israelite territory, David's contingent of troops had more success than the others (18:30). Alternatively, verse 30 may mean that David was wiser than the other officers—in tactical skills or management of men.

3. *Jonathan as mediator* (19:1-7)

Up to this point Saul alone had initiated threats or attacks on David; now he virtually ordered all the members of the court to join in finding a way to kill him. Jonathan, bound by a love covenant to David, could not allow his dear friend to be destroyed. First, he warned David to hide, apparently in a place known to them both—possibly a small cave (see comments below on 20:11-42). Then he proceeded to intercede with his father on David's behalf. Jonathan appealed to David's innocence in wrongdoing, his heroism in killing Goliath, and Saul's recognition that God had won a great victory for Israel through David. The king listened to Jonathan, and the death threat was withdrawn and reconciliation effected.

4. *Two more attempts on David's life* (19:8-17)

The reconciliation proved to be temporary. Verse 8 sets that stage for renewed threats on David's life. Evidently David's additional success against the Philistines stirred Saul's sense of insecurity of jealousy and threw him into another of his fits of depression. Apparently these attacks were becoming more severe. A second time music failed to alleviate his emotional disturbance, and a second time Saul tried to kill David with the javelin he was using as a scepter. This time David fled the palace and went to his own house. How he thought he would be safe there is not clear. He could have thought Saul soon would return to normal. Nor is it clear why his pursuers were to wait until morning to seize him or how Michal found out about the plan. But Michal did find out and persuaded David to flee. Though the text does not say so, the house was possibly on or in the town wall, thus facilitating an escape from the town (cf. Josh. 2:15; 2 Cor. 11:33). The men may have been waiting by the door at the front of the house when David escaped at the back of the house. After he got away, Michal fixed up his bed to look as if a person were in it.

Her possession of a "teraphim" (19:13; "image," "idol") in David's house raises some difficult questions. The idol may have been used as a sort of general good luck charm or a charm against barrenness. Michal and

David had not been married long, and it is entirely possible that David did not know the teraphim was in the house. Whatever its significance, it played its part in the ruse. In the morning when the men came to take David, Michal reported that he was ill and presumably let them glance into his room. The group went off to report to Saul the problem they faced. The king ordered that David's bed (a bedroll or a portable couch) be carried to the palace where David could be killed in bed. When the guard went in to pick up the bed, they discovered the ruse and returned to report to Saul. Perhaps they then took Michal back to the palace with them. When Saul rebuked Michal for letting David get away, she gave the excuse that he had threatened to kill her if she did not help him escape.

5. *David's flight to Ramah* (19:18–23)

All this delay and these comings and goings gave David time to make good his escape. Where could he go to be safe from so formidable a foe? The immediate answer was to Samuel, who had anointed him and who represented a force of opposition to Saul in the kingdom. Moreover, Samuel as a man of God should have some counsel for the harried fugitive. Ramah was only a little over fifteen miles north of Gibeah, and word soon got back to Saul that David was there. Saul then sent a small contingent to apprehend David. At this point divine intervention prevented the capture. As the soldiers approached the place where Samuel and David were, the Spirit of God fell on them and caused them to have some kind of ecstatic experience. Of course, they forgot all about the reason for which they had come. When the king heard what had happened, he sent a second squad to capture David; their experience was the same as that of the first group. A third platoon fell under the same power.

Saul, curious or exasperated or impatient, finally decided to go in person to try to impose his will on the situation. His inquiries concerning the whereabouts of Samuel and David led him to Naioth of Ramah, evidently a section of Ramah where presumably the school of the prophets lived. Saul too fell under the power of the Spirit, but his ecstatic experience put him into a trance that lasted for a good part of a twenty-four-hour span. The KJV rendering that he "lay down naked" (19:24) is probably not correct. More likely he removed only his outer robes and lay in his tunic; so the translation "He stripped off his robes" (v. 24 NIV) is preferable. Divine intervention prevented David's apprehension and death.

6. *David's parting from Jonathan* (20:1–42)

The confusion at Ramah gave David an opportunity to flee. Samuel possibly advised him to return to the court in case there was some chance of reconciliation. He may have had a slight hope that Saul's ecstatic experience at Ramah would effect some change in the king. And he especially

needed the counsel and support of his dearest friend. As he returned he
decided to make one last effort to discover the true intentions of Saul. If
that test revealed that king's determined hostility, he would have no
choice but to leave permanently.

David complained to Jonathan of Saul's purpose to kill him and asserted
his innocence of wrongdoing. Jonathan, possibly out of blindness brought
on by filial respect could not believe his father really had such intentions.
Moreover, he asserted that his father discussed his every move with him.
Whether Jonathan had been present when Saul attacked David is not
known. He perhaps dismissed what he knew about those attempts as
temporary emotional disturbances that were not reflective of a settled
determination in Saul's mind and heart. David was more perceptive,
however, and observed that Saul certainly knew something of their special friendship and therefore would not tell Jonathan what he really
thought about David. David said knowingly that there was literally "about
a step" (20:3) between him and death.

Then David proposed a test by which Saul's true intentions could be
determined. The next day would be the New Moon, which would be
celebrated by a religious and a civil festival (Num. 10:10; 28:11–15). This
two-day event would require David's presence at court, both because he
was now a high official in the administration and a member of the family.
He would deliberately absent himself, and the explanation of his absence
would be that his brother had requested him to be present for the annual
clan gathering in Bethlehem. If Saul passed off the matter lightly, it would
be known that he planned no mischief against David. But if he grew angry
and gave evidence of being denied his prey, his determination to destroy
David would be clear. Then, seeking to make sure Jonathan would grant
his request, David appealed to their love covenant made before God. If
he had really sinned against the house of Saul, he preferred that Jonathan
kill him rather than deliver him to his father. Jonathan swore that he
would indeed inform David if his father had designs on him.

When David asked how he would be notified of the outcome of the
proposed test if it were negative, Jonathan suggested that they go out into
"the field" (20:11), evidently the same field referred to in 1 Samuel
19:2–3. It is open to question as to why they went there when being seen
together in public was dangerous. Perhaps the reason was twofold: to
converse in absolute privacy and to agree on the means of informing
David about Saul's attitude toward him. This field presumably was the
one to the south of Gibeah, on the eastern edge of which were rocky
declivities where one could hide. It is almost certain that they did not sit
in the open field as they now conversed.

Jonathan did most of the talking and uttered one of the most selfless
statements ever made. First, he renewed his covenant with David, vow-
ing to tell him of his father's feelings toward him (20:12–13). Then, with a

certain premonition that David would become king, he begged David to make a perpetual covenant to protect him and his family. The tables were turned. Instead of David's fearing for his life, the line of Saul was begging for protection (20:14–16). Next, Jonathan made David swear again concerning his love (20:17). And last, he gave him the sign by which he would reveal Saul's attitude toward him (20:18–23). David apparently was to hide in the same place where he had hidden earlier (19:2–3).

The matter of hiding in the field requires further comment. In verse 5 David mentioned hiding in the field until the third evening. In verse 19 Jonathan referred to David's waiting for two days and then going down to hide himself. Verse 24 speaks about hiding in the field, presumably at the moment Jonathan and David parted. Coupled with this issue is the question of whether David had any intention of going to Bethlehem. Some commentators take the attitude that apparently David saw nothing wrong with telling a lie and simply fabricated the story of the family sacrificial feast in Bethlehem (v. 6). A way of reconciling all this is as follows. After Jonathan and David parted, David hid in the field for a while (20:24). Then apparently he left and went somewhere else; there was no food or water or clothing for him there. He may have gone to Bethlehem (20:6). Finally, he returned to his hiding place on the third night (two nights after their parting) or early the following morning to keep the appointment with Jonathan (20:19).

While David was absenting himself from the court, Jonathan was playing out his part in the test of Saul's intentions. The first day of the feast of the New Moon arrived. The members of the court filed in to eat. Apparently the most distinguished sat at a table for four in the corner. Saul sat with his back to the wall, perhaps both for security and so he could have a full view of the assembly. Verse 25 is difficult in the Hebrew. It seems to mean that Jonathan was sitting next to Saul; and when Abner came in, Jonathan got up and gave his place to the commander of the forces. Jonathan then sat opposite Saul, and there was an empty place for David across from Abner.

Saul was not upset over David's absence during the first day of the feast because he guessed that some ceremonial impurity may have kept him away. But on the second day the story was different. The king asked Jonathan about David's whereabouts, assuming that they kept in close contact. On hearing Jonathan's explanation, the king exploded. First, he hurled a striking Oriental form of abuse at him. To insult one's mother was one of the most cutting remarks anyone could utter. And, of course, the son as her offspring partook of her nature. Jonathan was viewed in the latter part of verse 30 as a disgrace to the womb. Second, Saul asserted that as long as David was alive, the throne was not safe. He portrayed David as a dangerous rival and ordered Jonathan to produce him so he could be killed. Third, when Jonathan asserted David's innocence, Saul in a rage flung his spear at his son and tried to kill him. The abusive language, the attack on his person, and the death sentence on his friend kindled Jonathan's "fierce anger" (20:34) and killed his appetite. And he probably spent a sleepless night.

In the morning he went out to the field to keep his appointment with David. As planned, he took a boy with him to retrieve his arrows during his archery practice. Verse 37 records the signal to David that Saul was bent on his destruction. The urgency in verse 38 was probably intended to prevent the boy from playing around as he collected the arrows and thus to happen on David's hiding place. But some take it as an instruction meant for David. Then the author makes it clear that the boy never discovered what had been going on. Jonathan had kept his agreement and delivered his message, but he apparently seized on one last chance to see David. He sent the boy back to town with his bow and quiver, and the covenant brothers bade a tearful farewell.

As David came out of his hiding place, he bowed three times in a gesture of homage to the king's son and perhaps to the sovereign workings of God. Jonathan made it clear that their covenant took precedence over the orders of the king and filial obedience; and he released David with the words, "Go in peace" (20:42). After a full flow of purest brotherly affection, the two parted; for all they knew, they might never meet again on earth.

Some critics are very dogmatic on the point that verses 41 and 42 do not belong in the text and are merely an editorial expansion. They feel that the account really concludes with verse 40 and an additional contact between David and Jonathan was too risky to be attempted. But they were alone and reasonably sure of the secrecy of their meeting, and two people who love each other very much often do run risks to say one last farewell.

For Further Study

1. Analyze the statements of David and Goliath made during their confrontation. Which may be regarded as utterance of truth or personal conviction and which were merely designed for propaganda warfare?

2. Write a newspaper account of the conflict between David and Goliath.

3. What elements may have been included in the love covenant between David and Jonathan? Write a love covenant between two modern believers.

4. Tabulate the attitudes toward David alluded to in this section and as expressed by Saul, Jonathan, Michal, Goliath, and the populace (court, village women, etc.).

Chapter 4

The Decline of Saul and the Rise of David (II) David's Wanderings and Saul's Death
(1 Samuel 21:1–31:13)

A. David's Wanderings (21:1–30:31)

1. *David at Nob* (21:1–9)

As David fled from the field at Gibeah, he was evidently in very dire straits. He presumably had not been able to return home after escaping out a window (19:12) and so had little or no baggage or food. Where should he go? The priestly village of Nob, a couple of miles away on the northern outskirts of Jerusalem, was a likely source of help. There, where the tabernacle was now located, both spiritual and material resources might be available. When David burst in on Ahimelech the priest, he frightened him, for Ahimelech could not imagine what emergency had arisen. Ahimelech (perhaps the same as Ahijah of 1 Sam. 14:3) was the great-grandson of Eli, high priest during Samuel's childhood. Since Mark 2:26 names Abiathar as priest instead of Ahimelech, his father, it may be that the two were acting in concert at this time.

David wanted to ensure assistance from the priest and also to protect Ahimelech against any punishment from Saul (as a result of the presence of Saul's servant Doeg, v. 7). Therefore David fabricated an account of a secret, or "urgent" (21:8), commission from Saul that had prevented adequate preparations for the trip. His falsehood and deception were to have disastrous consequences later (22:18–19). Though David's lie may have saved one life for the moment, the result of it was that scores of other lives would be snuffed out later on. David possibly had other "young men" (21:2 NASB) with him, or his mention of them merely may have been part of his story. The lack of reference to companions when he went to Gath (21:10–15) does not prove conclusively there were none, because the focus of attention then was on David. Nor does the reference to companions in Mark 2:26 provide final proof that David had men with him, because the priest may have thought he was giving the bread for others when actually there were none.

75

David asked for five loaves or cakes of bread or whatever else the priest might have. The response was that only consecrated bread was available—only bread that had been removed from the table of show-bread in the tabernacle when fresh bread was brought in. This was supposed to be reserved for the use of the priests (Lev. 24:9). Uncertain of what he should do, Ahimelech consulted the oracle of God (22:10) and received permission to release the bread, provided the men were ceremonially pure, i.e., had refrained from sexual relations (21:4; Exod. 19:15). David assured the priest that the young men's "things" (21:5 NIV; "vessels," NASB; i.e., their clothes and/or bodies were ceremonially clean even on an ordinary campaign; and they were especially so today. So Ahimelech gave David the bread, and a ritual ordinance yielded to the law of necessity.

Then David sought some sort of weapon, again pleading the urgency of his mission as the reason for being without his own weapons. Ahimelech observed that there was nothing on hand except the sword of Goliath, which evidently was kept in some elegant covering as a consecrated memorial. The phrase "whom you killed in the Valley of Elah" (21:9) perhaps indicates that David had better title to the sword than anyone else. So David left with food and a weapon. But there was a troublesome reference to Doeg the Edomite, overseer of the herdsmen of Saul. Doeg was "detained before Yahweh" (21:7), perhaps for the sake of purification or the fulfillment of a vow. This scoundrel is introduced here because of the part he will soon play in the massacre at Nob.

2. David at Gath (21:10–15)

It need not be assumed from verse 10 that on that very day David arrived in Gath. He tried to stay in Israel for a while but soon decided there was no way to do so. So he finally concluded that the only way to escape the long arm of Saul was to move to enemy territory. The NEB translation describes this process better: "That day, David went on his way, eluding Saul, and came to Achish king of Gath" (21:10). On the face of things, it might seem strange that David would even think he could be safe in Philistine territory after his victories over the Philistines. But the Philistines could easily congratulate themselves on winning over one of their most powerful foes. Various outstanding personalities have gone over to the enemy down through history; and certainly if one of the high officers of the Russian armed forces should defect, he would be welcomed in the United States. Achish, king of Gath, was seemingly disposed to receive David; but some of his courtiers were suspicious of him and were opposed to the action. Their classification of him as "king" (21:11) shows something of the high regard in which he was held by the Philistines and also their corresponding lack of respect for Saul.

Out of fear David feigned madness "in their hands" (21:13). The nobles had probably seized David and were pondering what to do with him. Verse 13 goes on to say that David "disguised his understanding," "scribbled" (NASB; "would drum," JB) on the city gate, and "let his saliva dribble down on his beard." An indignity to the beard was considered to be intolerable insult and would not have been permitted by a normal person. Evidently David put on a good act, and perhaps God helped him to be persuasive. The king did not want anyone like that around and apparently commanded that David be let go.

3. Wanderings in Judah and Moab (22:1-5)

David next moved to the area of Adullam, which is now commonly but not dogmatically located about twelve miles west-southwest of Bethlehem and thus about ten miles southeast of Gath. There he would have been in Judah, in the edge of territory controlled by the Israelites. When his father's family heard of it, they moved there for protection, for they could have been attacked at any time. David as an outlaw, by no choice of his and with no designs on the person of Saul, began to attract other outlaws and "man with a grievance" (22:2). Soon there were four hundred under his leadership.

Next David went east of the Dead Sea into the territory of Moab, possibly because he had Moabite blood in his veins (his great-grandmother was Ruth, Ruth 4:17, 22). More likely, however, he went there because he could expect protection as an opponent of a neighboring ruler. But it is entirely possible that David found a welcome for his parents at the court of the king of Moab because of Moabite kinship. The words "till I know what God will do for me" (22:3) show David's sense of God's sovereign control over his life and his resignation to the will of God. Some believe that the "stronghold" (22:4) was Masada, but others conclude that it was in Moab. In either case David would have been isolated from the people of Judah; he needed to be among them to build up a following. Hence the wisdom of the prophet Gad was evident when he counseled a return to the territory of Judah. Gad has not been heard of before, but he ministered to David on numerous occasions during his reign and will receive attention later. Perhaps he was sent by Samuel from the school of the prophets at Ramah. Obediently, David moved—to the forest of Hereth, location unknown.

4. Saul's war council and the Nob massacre (22:6-23)

David's renewed movements through Judah sent shock waves through the court and raised all kinds of bogies in the mind of Saul. From David's point of view, Saul sought his life and he must protect himself; from Saul's point of view, David was an outlaw and a serious threat to his throne. Saul called a meeting of the court, a kind of council of war. He sat enthroned with his spear as scepter. He first appealed to the cupidity and tribal jealousy of his hearers. Saul had evidently chosen Benjamites as courtiers; he insinuated that they would not enjoy the privileges they now had under a monarch from the tribe of Judah (David). Next he pulled out the crying towel and enjoyed a bit of self-pity. Then he condemned the friendship between Jonathan and David and interpreted the actions of Jonathan as an incitement to rebellion. In fact, he asserted that Jonathan had something to do with the present moves of David. Interestingly, Jonathan did not appear with Saul again until he died with him in battle (1 Sam. 31:2). When Saul complained that no one at court had come forth with information about the relationship of these two friends, he opened the door for anyone to divulge information of military or administrative value.

Doeg, who previously seems to have had no real access to the king, though he was on the adminstrative staff, stepped forward and reported that Ahimelech the priest had given aid and comfort to the enemy. Saul immediately sent for the whole priestly family to come from Nob. Since Nob was a couple of miles away and it would have taken some time to assemble the whole group at Gibeah, there must have been a considerable recess before the kangaroo court scene of verses 12–18 could occur. Saul hurled the accusation at Ahimelech. But the priest replied that he had often inquired of God on David's behalf and that he knew nothing about the feud between Saul and David. Why should he be suspicious of David, who was a highly respected member of the royal staff and the king's son-in-law! Somehow the ruse by which David obtained the priest's help never surfaced; it was possibly not yet fully understood. Ahimelech and the rest of the priests were judged guilty of being party to conspiracy.

Saul now had sunk so low as to command the death of the servants of God. When he gave the order for their execution, the king's men stood stunned and motionless. An alien Edomite finally carried out the sacrilegious sentence. He presumably did not do it alone but had some help in killing the eighty-five priests. Then, in an effort to terrify all opponents of Saul who might give aid to David, the king commissioned Doeg to obliterate completely the population of Nob and their possessions. Thus the judgment on the house of Eli was completely fulfilled (2:27–36). One son of Ahimelech, Abiathar, escaped and fled to David with the sacred vestments. He became priest and David's close associate. David confessed his guilt in bringing on this grisly tragedy and urged Abiathar to remain with him. David's statement, "You will be safe with me," reflected his belief in divine deliverance and accession to the throne. The action of Saul, just reported to him, was that of a desperate man whose decline was becoming more evident.

5. *Rescue of Keilah* (23:1–13)

It would be a mistake to view the latter chapters of 1 Samuel as merely a string of events in the life of David while he wandered in the desert trying to escape the long arm of Saul. They beautifully portray the faithfulness of God to the one He had chosen to become king and His refinement and training of that candidate for the royal office. Moreover, they show how David's many interventions on behalf of his people prepared them to accept him as monarch. And they describe the personal and administrative slippage of Saul as he became increasingly obsessed with David's threat to his throne.

After David's return to the highlands of Judah, he received a report of Philistine incursions against Keilah, less than five miles south of the probable site of Adullam. These attacks were particularly troublesome because they involved looting the threshing floors filled with ripened grain. The plundering threatened to reduce the people to virtual starvation. To rescue the people of Keilah would be a humane act, but there was a very real question as to whether David should march against the enemies of the state without orders from the king.

So he inquired of God, probably through Abiathar's use of the Urim and Thummim. The answer was in the affirmative, but his men were reticent. When they were not safe from Saul's pursuit, how could they take on the Philistines as well? A second inquiry brought the command, "Go down to Keilah" and the promise of victory, "I will give the Philistines into your hand" (23:4). So they promptly responded and rescued the people of Keilah. Verse 6 explains how the ephod of the high priest with the Urim and Thummim came to be in the camp of David. However, verse 6 complicates matters by saying that Abiathar fled to David at Keilah, when 22:20 implies he came into David's company before reaching Keilah. The Septuagint text avoids this problem, saying, "And it came to pass when Abiathar the son of Ahimelech fled to David, that he went down with David to Keilah, having an ephod in his hand."

When Saul heard about David's foray, he concluded that David had walked into a trap: he was in a city with walls and gates where he could be shut up like a bird in a cage and besieged and captured. Saul's statement that "God has rejected and delivered him into my hand" (23:7) showed that Saul still failed to comprehend that he himself was the one whom God had rejected. Saul sent out an order to muster the troops, at least from the adjoining area, no doubt on the pretext of fighting the Philistines. But David knew that Saul secretly "was forging mischief against him" (23:9) and he again inquired of God. The answer he got was that Saul would indeed besiege Keilah and threaten to destroy it in order to force the people to surrender David and his men. The inhabitants would give up to save themselves. This revelation sounds like horrible ingratitude after what David had just done for them, but no doubt the memory of the Nob massacre was fresh in the minds of the people of Keilah. They knew Saul was perfectly capable of pulling down the walls, burning the city, and killing all its inhabitants. David and his force, which had now grown to six hundred, withdrew from Keilah and wandered about.

6. Wandering in the wilderness of Ziph (23:14–28)

Saul gave up the attack on Keilah and pursued David into the Wilderness of Ziph, but God's hand of protection was on him. The town of Ziph was about three to four miles southeast of Hebron; and the Wilderness of Ziph was that part of the Wilderness of Judea to the east of the town between Ziph and the Dead Sea. In ancient times there was in that desert an area known as Horesh (meaning "thicket"). Evidently the area was overgrown with brushwood although no trace of these scrub trees exists today.

Saul went home while David was in Horesh, but Jonathan heard where David was and at great personal risk located his beloved friend. Jonathan "strengthened his hand in God" (23:16 KJV), i.e., strengthened David's heart by his assurances and renewal of the covenant. There is no certainty from what is said that either Jonathan or Saul knew anything of David's anointing. But it had become evident to Jonathan from the course of events that Saul's fortunes were declining and David's were rising; David's accession to the throne became ever more certain. Jonathan asserted that deep down in his heart Saul had reached the same conclusion. What a magnificent person Jonathan must have been! And how great must have been his victory over natural feelings and ambitions! With calm assurance he could talk of his dearest friend's taking over the kingdom he should have inherited. And in loving self-denial he could request the second place in the kingdom. He had certainly learned to bow before what he believed to be the sovereign will of God with complete peace of mind. Once more the two renewed the covenant by solemn oath; and they parted, never to see each other again on earth.

In striking contrast to Jonathan's support of David is the Ziphite betrayal of him. Ziph stood at an altitude of almost twenty-nine hundred feet above sea level and about one hundred feet above the surrounding region. The inhabitants could presumably command a view of the area that included occasional glimpses of David's men. It is possible they feared depredations by David's lawless band, and they may have been uneasy about the ability of the slender resources of the region to support both themselves and David's entourage. It is conceivable too that David levied protection money against them. For whatever reason, they decided to surrender David to Saul. Saul thanked them for their compassion because he believed David had murderous intentions against him. Then he instructed them to reconnoiter carefully David's movements while he organized a military force to come and seize him. The location of Hakilah is unknown and Jeshimon probably is not a proper name but a word for wasteland located along the western side of the Dead Sea.

When the Ziphite company left the court of Saul and preceded him southward, they learned that David had moved farther south and east to Maon and the desert east of the town. The site of Maon is now called Khirbet Ma'in, eight miles south of Hebron. In hot pursuit Saul moved in on David and was about to pounce on him when a breathless messenger urged him to come away immediately because the Philistines were on the warpath again. David was saved.

From what is said about David's actions in the last several chapters of 1 Samuel, it should not be concluded that he was afraid to fight, or that he was out to destroy Saul. He was not a party to civil war in Israel; he and his men were not trying to topple the government. They only sought to protect themselves against the threats and depredations of the government. Nor did David wish to have anything to do with regicide, as numerous encounters between him and Saul indicate. If David's tough warriors had taken on Saul and his men, they possibly could have destroyed them; but David would not lift his hand against the Lord's anointed, and he had no desire to spill the blood of fellow Israelites.

7. David in the wilderness of En Gedi (23:29–24:22)

While Saul was off fighting the Philistines, David moved to the wilderness of En Gedi. There, midway along the western side of the Dead Sea, a copious spring sends its waters plunging toward the sea, six hundred feet below. A beautiful waterfall and a pool large enough for many to bathe in at a time present a welcome sight to hot and weary travelers in a thirsty land. The waters are still sufficient to create an oasis, and a modern Israeli kibbutz takes advantage of the fertile soil and the water to irrigate it. Wild goats lived nearby on the crags in ancient times, and caves provided sheepfolds and living space for people such as David's band.

After his campaign against the Philistines, Saul pursued David in this wild and desolate region. His force of three thousand must have represented the standing army or the military force regularly available to Saul. The same number was employed again in 26:2, and it was the number Saul recruited at the beginning of his kingship (13:2).

At a certain point in the expedition, Saul went into a cave alone to perform the necessities of nature, not for a siesta, as some have concluded. This happened to be the very cave in which David and at least some of his men were positioned. Saul, coming into the dark from blazing sunlight, did not have eyes accommodated to the darkness as David did. Moreover, he could be seen silhouetted at the mouth of the cave but could not peer into its inner recesses. Evidently he took off his outer cloak and laid it down near the entrance and went into one of the side chambers of the cave. Men and animals presumably were making enough noise outside so David's footsteps in going to the robe and cutting off a piece of it were not heard.

The assertion of David's men that this was the day of which the Lord had spoken (24:4) was not true. In the first place there is no record in Scripture that God would deliver Saul into David's hand. Second, David's declaration that he could not stretch out his hand against the Lord's anointed denies it. Third, his continued opposition to harming Saul and his determination to let God execute whatever judgment was to be meted out are decisive. His men probably concluded that the divine providence that had brought Saul into his hand was to be considered a message from God that he should take this opportunity to kill his enemy. Even the cutting off of a piece of Saul's robe left David conscience-smitten, for harming Saul's clothing seemed tantamount to harming his person; and he refused to let his men touch Saul.

With the courage that derives from innocence, David called after Saul when he was some distance from the mouth of the cave. As Saul turned around, David prostrated himself in true Oriental fashion to show his profound respect for the king's authority. Then he complained of Saul's acceptance of the slander of evil advisers who claimed that David intended to harm the king. Next he declared that his innocence of such charges was to be proved from events of this day. Saul had been in his power in the cave and he could have killed him. To prove he could have done so, he held up the piece he had cut from the king's robe. In calling Saul "my father" (24:11), David expressed childlike reverence and affection, and he possibly alluded to the fact that Saul was his father-in-law. David would refuse to lay a hand on the king, God's anointed, who therefore was sacrosanct. Instead, he would leave his cause in the hands of God.

David tried to buttress his argument further by quoting an ancient proverb: "Out of the wicked comes forth wickedness" (24:13 NASB). The point of this is that only a wicked man would seek revenge; he did not, and his motives were pure. Finally, David wanted to present himself as harmless, as no threat to the monarch: A dead dog cannot bite. A single flea is utterly insignificant. In the light of all these points of David's argument, Saul had no good reason for persecuting David, who would fearlessly appeal to God for justice.

David's presentation of his case totally disarmed Saul. Overcome with emotion, he "wept aloud" (24:16) in Oriental fashion. Affectionately calling David "my son" (v. 16) he acknowledged David's righteousness in sparing his life. He even invoked God's blessing on David and confirmed what Jonathan had said about his father's realizing that the kingdom would be David's. And he, like Jonathan, asked David to make a solemn oath to spare his family. For the moment Saul's feelings were completely altered and he was able even to bestow a sincere blessing on the one who would supplant his dynasty. Release from his emotional disorder led him to abandon his attack on David and thus to spare the latter. But David was wise enough to realize that this change in feelings was only temporary; so he remained in the "stronghold" (24:22), the mountainous part of the Desert of Judea.

8. *David, Nabal, and Abigail* (25:1–44)

The chapter begins with a reference to the death of Samuel, some would say because it happened then and others because it had a connection with the removal of David from En Gedi. According to the latter view, the death of Samuel lifted all restraint from Saul in his treatment of David; so David and his men moved once more to escape the long arm of the king. But it seems more likely that David's real reason for moving at this time was the need to find provisions for his numerous followers.

Whenever he died, Samuel received proper tribute from a grateful people. They held a national period of mourning for an extended period of time, as if the flag hung at half-staff for thirty days. Then they buried him "in his house" (25:1), evidently on the grounds adjacent to the house and possibly in a specially constructed mausoleum. No person had been so important in the history of Israel since the days of Moses and Joshua. His personal piety, his moral and spiritual reform, his institution of the schools of the prophets, his leadership in defeat of the Philistines, his impeccable record in judicial activity, and his function as kingmaker all helped to give him the eminent place he held in the history of the nation and the hearts of the people.

Where David moved from En Gedi is a debated question. The Hebrew text says the "wilderness of Paran" (25:1), on the border between Canaan and the Sinai. If so, the distance he traveled would have been at least a hundred miles. Of course, it is possible that he went that far (though distances in 1 Samuel generally are rather minute); and the region offered employment for his men, who could protect livestock on the extensive pasture lands during grazing season. But the rest of the chapter indicates that he was reasonably close to Carmel and Maon. The Septuagint reading of the latter part of 25:1 stipulates that he moved to the wilderness, or desert of Maon, and the NIV and JB follow that reading. It would be natural for him to move from the region along the shore of the Dead Sea back into the highlands of Judea. And the events of chapter 26 locate David and his men just to the north of Carmel and Maon.

Those who have a low view of the inspiration of Scripture and/or those who put undue stress on the Bible as literature often like to characterize this chapter as merely a romantic tale of how David came to marry Abigail. It is that, but it also is much more. It gives insights into the means by which David supported his substantial company and even the character of that company. It shows the humanness of David under stress and his capability to commit a great atrocity in a fit of anger. But preeminently it shows the watchful care of God in preserving him from an act of

passion that might have endangered his calling to be king and of providing
for him something of a base for social and economic acceptance in Judah.
And it gives another indication that he would indeed be king someday.

The principal characters in this drama, besides David, were Nabal and
his wife Abigail. Nabal was a very wealthy resident of Maon who also
owned property at Carmel, about a mile away. Both towns were located
about eight miles southeast of Hebron. As was common in those days,
Nabal's wealth was reckoned largely in terms of livestock: a thousand
goats and three thousand sheep. Nabal was "surly and evil in his deal-
ings," and Abigail was "intelligent and beautiful" (25:3). Nabal's name
means "fool" in the sense of one who has no understanding of what is right
and proper. If the fact that he was a Calebite means he was of the family of
Caleb, then he was of the tribe of Judah, as David was. But many take
Caleb ("dog") to be a common noun instead of a proper noun and describe
him as "snappish as a dog."

Act 1 of this drama took place at a spring sheep-shearing at Carmel.
Such an event was a festival, as were harvest and grape gathering; and
generosity, hospitality, and feasting were customary (cf. 25:36; 2 Sam.
13:23, 28). In both ancient and modern Canaan, favors often were asked
and accounts settled at sheep-shearings. In this context David sent ten
men to Nabal with a request. In effect, they were asking for "protection
money," compensation for all the services rendered in helping to care for
Nabal's livestock during previous months. Sometimes Bedouins or other
migrants were guilty of a form of extortion when they demanded payment
for simply refraining from harm to a shepherd. In this case, however,
service was real and expectation of payment justified.

The ten men evidently went to Nabal with the hope of a generous gift.
Bulky and heavy payments made in kind in a primitive society often
required numerous individuals to carry them. David instructed his young
men to greet Nabal in a friendly manner (25:6; with a wish for long life and
good fortune). They were to remind him of their services and to urge him
to give "whatever your hand finds" (25:8; as much as you can) to them and
"your son David" (v. 8; thereby expressing fatherly goodwill). Nabal's
reply was insolent and sarcastic in tone ("he hurled insults," v. 14) and
selfish in character (he withheld "my food and drink," v. 11). The reply
was negative in content and indicative of social and political disintegration
("many tear away from their masters" v. 10). Instead of recognizing David
as the future king of Israel, as Abigail was to do, Nabal classified him as a
runaway slave.

In Act 2, Scene 1, David's men reported the rebuff to their leader, and
David lost his temper and ordered his men to arm themselves and accompany him. The action was ominous, but it was not yet quite clear what he
intended to do. Under the circumstances, David's protection of Nabal's
property established a claim to tribute or compensation; and when with-

held the claim could be enforced as a right. Of course David's men could not leave their possessions unguarded; so two hundred stayed at the camp. Later (ch. 30) it was legally determined that such persons also have a right to whatever booty was seized.

Scene 2 reveals a state of alarm in Maon. One of the servants reported the whole nasty confrontation at Carmel. The servant rehearsed the true service David and his men had rendered ("they were a wall around us" [25:16] in protecting against marauders and wild animals). He predicted "disaster" (v. 17 NIV) if something was not done immediately. Evidently the servant gathered that retribution would follow from the way Nabal had acted and from the manner in which the ten members of David's camp had departed. The servant knew it would do no good to appeal to Nabal to appease David, for Nabal was "a wicked man" (25:17; "son of Belial" KJV). He was worthless and vicious, and "no one can reason with him" (v. 17). Abigail went into action immediately, putting together a considerable gift for David: two hundred bread cakes, two goatskins filled with wine, five dressed sheep, five seahs (about a bushel) of roasted grain, one hundred raisin cakes, and two hundred cakes of dried figs. Like Jacob of old (Gen. 32:13–21), she decided to soften up her antagonist by sending the gift on ahead of her.

Act 3 opens with a height of dramatic intensity; a lone apprehensive woman rides behind a donkey caravan loaded with gifts. As she reaches the brow of a hill and descends the other side, David with his force of four hundred begins to descend the hill opposite, fuming with indignation and determined to exterminate all the males of Nabal's household. The sacred historian now reveals his true intent (25:22). What will happen as the two meet in the valley below?

What occurs in one of the finest speeches to persuade ever delivered (freshman speech students take note). First she established the proper atmosphere for it. By dismounting in the presence of a superior, she was showing homage to David. Then she demonstrated further respect by prostrating herself before him. Thus by her actions she made amends for the disrespect of her husband. Next Abigail took Nabal's guilt on herself and hoped that David would not avenge it on her. Throughout her speech she expressed her own humility and implied David's magnanimity. As a matter of fact, she observed, Nabal was a fool and did not know what was right and proper anyway; so a wise person should pay no attention to him. As for herself (who did know what was right), she had not seen the ten young men to give them their just deserts.

In the next division of her speech (25:26–27), Abigail used three arguments, each introduced by the same Hebrew construction, to put David in a frame of mind to accept her appeal for forgiveness. First, she observed that by her actions God had kept him from "shedding blood" and from "avenging yourself" (25:26 NASB). The intimation was that he had already agreed to abandon his attack on Nabal. In the act of murder he would have sinned against God, would have brought a horrible blight of guilt on his own conscience, and would have embroiled his house in a blood feud in which vengeance would be taken on him. Second, she pointed out in the latter part of verse 26 that God was the real Avenger. Folly, of the sort exemplified by Nabal, brings down the punishment of God (cf. Deut. 32:35; Rom. 12:19). Clearly, she was pronouncing doom on her husband. Third, she offered her "gift" (25:27; literally "blessing") because it expressed good will and implied a request that it be accepted as proof of David's forgiveness.

Then, finally, Abigail made a specific request for forgiveness. But the shrewd woman immediately supported her plea with the general argument that a successful man can afford to be magnanimous. She noted that success is seen first in God's making a "firmly established house" (25:28; "lasting dynasty") for David. Her belief in God's choice of David as king of Israel amounts almost to a prophecy and anticipates the Davidic covenant (2 Sam. 7). Her certainty of his accession to the throne (25:30) almost implies her knowledge of his anointing.

Second, success was assured because of the protecting shield of Providence. Though the attacks of his enemies would come, God would bind him "securely in the bundle of the living" (25:29 NIV). This is a reference to a bundle in which an Israelite householder securely tied together silver and other precious belongings. That protecting care would not extend to his enemies, whom God would "hurl away as from the cup [or 'pocket'] of a sling" (v. 29).

Third, the success of David's administration would be enhanced because he would not labor under the burden of a guilty conscience or blood guilt that brings inevitable retribution. Though protected from that now, David was to suffer from blood guilt during the latter part of his administration (2 Sam. 12:10). Then Abigail tucked in a concluding thought: a request that David would remember her when he achieved the predicted greatness.

What a persuasive speech from a beautiful and intelligent woman! David was deeply moved. And judging from subsequent events, the impression she made was profound. David's reply involved first, praise to God for having sent Abigail; second, congratulations to Abigail, who had kept him from bloodshed; and third, acceptance of the gifts with the assurance of pardon.

Scene 2 takes place back in Maon. Abigail has returned home to find Nabal at his sheep-shearing feast and dead drunk. He was in no condition to hear about the events of the day. The following morning when he was sober, Abigail gave him a full account. As he was still suffering from a hangover, the shock was too much for his system; and evidently he had a stroke that paralyzed him. It is not clear what affected Nabal most: his near brush with death, his loss of substance, or his total humiliation before David. Perhaps all contributed to it. Ten days later Nabal had another seizure and died. It is not necessary to conclude that David expressed vindictive glee over the death of Nabal. Perhaps he was thankful that God had executed vengeance and had saved him from blood guilt.

Scene 3 takes its setting at Maon a few days later. In true Oriental form, David sent for a woman who pleased him to come and be his wife. And Abigail had no choice but to comply. Judging from her earlier statements about his anticipated greatness, she found it reasonably easy to join him. The fact that she did implies a higher degree of comfort in David's camp than generally is thought. Moreover, David already "had . . . taken" (25:43 NASB) Ahinoam of Jezreel, about six miles southwest of Hebron, as his wife; and conceivably others of his six hundred men also had married. So the drama closes with a changing perspective on the camp of David. For the moment his first wife, Michal, has been given to another, but she will be restored to him later (2 Sam. 3:13–16). Even before ascending to the throne, David has fallen into the polygamous practices of other Near Eastern monarchs.

9. *David's second sparing of Saul* (26:1–25)

Critics commonly find it difficult or impossible to conceive of David's sparing Saul twice or of the Ziphites' betraying David twice. So they try to view chapters 24 and 26 as separate accounts of the same event. To be sure, there are a few superficial similarities, such as Saul's pursuing with three thousand men, David's sparing Saul, and Saul's having some sort of grief over his animosity toward David. But almost everything else in the accounts is different. The geographical locations differ, with one taking place at En Gedi and the other in the area of Ziph; one account occurs during the day and the other at night; one occurs in a cave and the other in a camp; in one the cloak is cut and in the other possessions are carried off; in one there seems to be genuine remorse and in the other only some casual recognition of the blessing of God on David. The list of disparities goes on. The evidence all seems to lead to the conclusion that these chapters record two different events.

It may be asked why David would return to the general vicinity of Ziph when the people of the region had betrayed him once. He possibly felt that Saul had moderated toward him and it was safe now, but more likely he rather naturally found himself in this general vicinity. Ziph was about four miles southeast of Hebron, and Carmel and Maon were another four miles farther southeast. His care of Abigail's livestock probably took him up to a couple of miles north of Carmel, and that is about where the Ziphites reported he was. If the reason for betraying him before was their worry about his encroachment on their resources and their territory, that threat was even greater now that he owned property in the area.

After the Ziphites called on Saul to come south from Gibeah, he arrived with three thousand men, evidently the standing army encamped at the capital. David sent out scouts to reconnoiter Saul's movements and camp location. Then he himself went to spy out the camp, which was located on a small flat-topped hill. Evidently he looked into the camp from an adjacent higher hill. To strike camp, the army had put equipment and animals and possibly some carts in a circle; and the men, without tents, slept on the ground inside that perimeter. In the safest place at the very center lay the king and Abner, commander of the forces. Stuck in the ground by the king's head stood his spear as scepter. Probably a small fire and possibly some oil lamps were kept burning all night. Thus the camp was somewhat illuminated and David could watch unobserved from the darkness above. His movements may have been aided by the moonlight. Apparently no sentries were posted because there was no threat of attack by David as there would have been by a foreign enemy.

David devised some sort of plan. Exactly what he intended to do is not clear; he could not have known in advance that God would prosper his venture by bringing a supernatural sleep on the camp. It is possible he had the high priest inquire of God if he should go into the camp. In any event what he did required magnificent courage; and he got Abishai to volunteer to go with him. Abishai and Joab were brothers and their mother was Zeruiah, David's sister (1 Chron. 2:16); so Abishai was David's nephew.

Where the conversation of 26:8-11 took place is not clear. It hardly seems possible that the pair would have dared even to whisper while standing over Saul and Abner. Perhaps they talked on the hillside above the camp. Wherever it took place, it involved the desire of Abishai to kill Saul and David's refusal to lay a finger on God's anointed. God would have to strike him or he would die a natural death or die in battle. David wanted only to make off with Saul's spear and the water flask that normally hung around Saul's neck as he traveled, but now lay alongside his spear. A "deep sleep" (26:12) sent by the Lord made the venture possible and shows divine approval of it. God could approve this expedition because David's conduct was God-honoring throughout. By these efforts David again wanted to remonstrate with Saul about the injustice of his attacks on his innocent servant.

After making off with the spear and the flask, David and Abishai climbed the hill at some distance from the camp and called to Abner and the army. The accoustical qualities of the mountainous regions of Palestine are excellent; and, of course, they are even better at night when the competing sounds of the day are still. At length Abner woke up and responded, "Who . . . shouts to the king?" (26:14; i.e., who calls to the king's representative or who disturbs the king with his shouting?). Then David taunted and chided Abner for his dereliction of duty that put the king's life in jeopardy and that therefore should have resulted in court martial and execution of Abner and his military police detail. As proof of Abner's failure, David directed Abner to see if he could find the king's spear and water jug.

At that point Saul, recognizing David's voice but unable to see his form, broke into the conversation. Thus David had his chance to put his case before the king. First he declared his innocence of wrongdoing. Then he suggested two possible causes of Saul's hostility. The first was that God may have stirred up Saul against David. This could be dealt with by the offering of acceptable sacrifices, perhaps on the part of both of them. The second possible cause was that men (advisers) may have turned the heart of the king. This could be dealt with by levying a curse on them. What they had done was very serious indeed; they were about to drive him from the land of Israel. In this other territory where there was no shrine to Yahweh, one was separated from the people of God and subject to the seductions of other gods.

In fact, it was so common for peoples of the ancient Near East to view their gods as controlling or being especially related only to the little turf of the tribe or nation that the Israelites fell into this same mind-set. Few of them, like Isaiah, could perceive of Yahweh as God of the nations and capable of caring for His people wherever they found themselves. This fact made the exile in Assyria and Babylonia an even more bitter experience when it occurred.

David now shuddered at the thought of operating outside the special sphere of the rule of Yahweh. Furthermore, he found it repugnant that if he died a violent death on foreign soil, his blood would not be avenged (26:20). Saul's searching for a "flea" emphasized David's insignificance. David's being hunted as a "partridge" referred to the manner of taking one's prey. The way a partridge was hunted was to keep following it around, constantly rousing it from its hiding place. Then when it was totally exhausted, it was brought down by hitting it with sticks and stones. No doubt David felt very much like a partridge at the moment.

Once more Saul was brought to the point of confession and once more promised not to harm David. But this time there were no tears; the confession was rather perfunctory, and there was no evidence of steps taken to alter a pattern of life. After David's indirect pronouncement of a blessing on himself, not tooting his own horn but a testimony of a good conscience before God (26:23–24), Saul uttered a forced acknowledgement of David's ultimate success: "You will . . . surely prevail" (v. 25 NASB). This time there was not mention of David's taking the kingdom. The whole tenor of Saul's conduct gave evidence that this heart was much more hardened than before.

By this time there probably was enough light in the sky so David could hold up the king's spear and invite someone to come over and get it. The two parted, with Saul going back to Gibeah with his three thousand and David continuing as an outlaw, not daring to do anything else. A teasing question, not dealt with here, is what Saul's army thought of these proceedings; they heard every word of the conversation between Saul and David. Moreover, one wonders about what Saul said to Abner for his dereliction of duty in failing to protect the king. And did Abner lose face before his men as a result of the jibes of David?

10. *David among the Philistines* (27:1–12)

Soon after that David did indeed feel that Saul's actions were driving him from "the LORD'S inheritance" (26:19), and he fled to Philistine territory for safety. His destination was Gath and the court of Achish. Whether this was the same Achish to whom David had resorted earlier (21:10) must be left open to question. This Achish is described as the son or descendant of Maoch and the other was not, but that fact does not prove the two were different. How much time elapsed between 1 Samuel 21 and 27 is not clear, but possibly this Achish was a son of the earlier man by the same name.

Whether or not he was the same, the question must be asked why David was accepted on this occasion but not on the former one. Perhaps the reason is that the circumstances were completely different. On the earlier occasion David was an Israelite hero who had just killed Goliath, and he was weak and had little to offer the Philistines. Now he was a well-known fugitive from the king of Israel, an archenemy of the Philistines. Moreover, David had a formidable force that might be used against the Israelites. It even may be suspected that Achish invited David to join him when he saw that the split between David and Saul could be used to his advantage. Even if Achish did not invite David to join him, it is likely that some fairly extensive negotiations preceded David's movement into Philistia.

At any rate David came with his six hundred men and their wives and children. What could be surmised on the basis of 25:43 (see comment above) is now made clear and specific, namely, that many of David's followers were marrying and/or bringing the wives they already had to the camp (cf. 30:3). David's two wives were part of the large community that moved across the border. Nothing further is said of Abigail's property. Perhaps it was sold off or held for her by relatives in the area of Carmel or seized by Saul. The move had its desired effect; Saul gave up the pursuit of David.

David's residence in Gath was unsatisfactory from every standpoint. The crowding of six hundred new families into a town already well populated must have caused severe housing problems and a considerable amount of friction with the native population over employment and other economic and social issues. Philistine suspicion of Israelite loyalty must have been great, as was the risk of contamination of Yahweh worship by Philistine idolatry. Then there was the danger of ultimate assimilation of the Hebrews into the Philistine populace. Finally, David's own style was cramped.

So David requested the privilege of living in a village in the country, a move that would go a long way toward solving the many issues raised above. Preeminently, the Israelites could live together as a community and maintain their worship; and David would have a headquarters from which he could launch his raids and build his power base. Achish responded with the gift of Ziklag. The site is not definitely located, but it is now thought to have been at Tell esh-Shania, some fifteen miles northwest of Beersheba and about twenty-five miles south of Gath. The site had been assigned to Simeon after the conquest (Josh. 19:5; 1 Chron. 4:30) but evidently was later taken over by the Philistines. Perhaps it was virtually uninhabited at the time Achish gave it to David, and he may have given it to David to establish an outpost of power and order in that unruly region.

During the year and four months David lived in Ziklag, he was involved in several raids. The historian refers to raids against the Geshurites, who occupied an area to the southwest (cf. Josh. 13:2); the Girzites, otherwise unknown; and the Amalekites, who were marauders along the southern border after Saul's victories over them (cf. 15:8–9). All of these seem to have been nomads living along the border between Canaan and Egypt. Evidently the occasions for David's military actions were plundering incursions made by these people against the south of Israel. In defense of the Israelites, David would take off after these raiders and exterminate them and take their livestock as booty, thus gaining the good will of the people of Judah and sustenance for his growing community.

He commonly returned to report to Achish after these raids and perhaps even shared a little of the booty with him (27:9). When Achish asked him where he had been raiding, he would say, "Against the south of Judah," or "the south of Jerahmeel," or "the south of the Kenites" (27:10; the latter two were districts associated with tribes linked to Judah). Thus the reports were deliberately deceptive and misleading. David meant for his answers to indicate the direction he had gone. Achish took them to mean that David's raids were against Israelite territory when actually they were against the enemies of Israel at their southern border. Achish thought David was building animosity against himself in the hearts of Israelites; instead, David was buying favor and building a base of acceptance in preparation for the day when he would be hailed king of Judah. No doubt David defended his devastating and cruel raids as acts of self-defense on behalf of his people. Achish finally convinced himself that David was becoming so totally alienated from his people that his band would make an excellent integral part of the Philistine army. And he wanted to join them to his forces during the imminent contest with Saul.

11. *Saul's fate pronounced* (28:1-25)

While David was living in Philistine territory, the Philistines mustered their troops for a campaign against Israel. Undoubtedly the time seemed right for such an attempt. Samuel, who had provided a rallying point against them, was dead. David, the great leader in warfare against them, had gone over to the other side. The grasp of Saul on the helm of government had slackened, and morale was low in Israel. Perhaps to test David or possibly just to inform him, Achish let him know he was expected to fight on the Philistine side. Now it became evident to David what a truly great predicament he had put himself in by taking up residence among the Philistines. What he really thought about the prospect of fighting his own people is never revealed; neither is the reader informed about what he told his troops before they marched off to battle (29:2). Fortunately, he never had to choose between the alternatives of defection from the Philistine army and fighting the troops of Saul.

David's response to Achish was a studied ambiguity: "You will see . . . what your servant can do" (28:2). Achish could take this as a promise of heroic deeds on behalf of the Philistines, but the statement could just as easily apply to defection or fifth column activity. "Your servant" is only an indication of respect for a superior. Achish was delighted with what he thought was a commitment to loyal service and promoted David to "keeper of my head" or "captain of my bodyguard," meaning that Achish entrusted his personal safety to David.

As the Philistines threatened Israel this time, they did not invade Judah in the south or the central theater, where Saul's power was concentrated, but moved up into northern Israel. Marching across the Valley of Jezreel (Esdraelon), they set up camp at Shunem, seven miles east of Megiddo on the southwest slope of the hill of Moreh. The Israelites camped just across a narrow valley to the south of them on the northern slope of Mount Gilboa. Mount Gilboa is a range of hills about eight miles long at the southeast edge of the Valley of Jezreel. Standing to an altitude of about sixteen hundred feet, Gilboa merges with the central uplands of Samaria to the south. Between Gilboa and Moreh is a valley leading from Jezreel to Beth Shan, a strategic fortress guarding the most important Jordan River crossing.

As Saul watched the Philistine build-up, he became increasingly terrified about what to do or what the future held for him. He sought a word from God but none came; the heavens were as brass. God did not answer by any of the usual means: by revelation in a dream, or the Urim and Thummim, or some word through a prophet. No vision from the Lord was given him. He had killed off the priestly group at Nob, and the high priest had fled to David with the sacred vestments, including the Urim and Thummim. Even if a new high priest had been appointed, God presumably refused to answer any inquiry made through him. Samuel had turned his back on him and later died; probably no other member of the school of the prophets paid any attention to the king either.

In this desperation Saul decided to turn for help to the occult—to necromancy (consulting the dead)—in order to determine the future. Such a practice was strictly forbidden in the Mosaic Law (Lev. 19:31; 20:6; Deut. 18:10–11). Anyone who consulted "familiar spirits," was to be killed (Lev. 20:6 KJV), and the one who conjured up such spirits was to be stoned to death (Lev. 20:27). There were periodic attempts to stamp out necromancy in Israel, and Saul himself had made an effort to do so (28:3, 9; cf. 2 Kings 23:24). But the prohibition of a popular religious practice does not abolish it; and when Saul decided to engage in it, his attendants were able to find a spiritistic medium within reasonable distance at Endor.

Endor stood on the north side of the hill of Moreh, north of the Philistine lines. The town was some ten miles north of Saul's camp. Saul's willingness to make the perilous night journey around the Philistine forces shows something of his desperation. He and his two companions disguised themselves for the double purpose of protection against any Philistines they might meet and to conceal the king's identity from the medium. When Saul arrived and made his request, he had great difficulty getting the woman to comply. She feared that she was being caught in a trap by agents of Saul, who sought to destroy her too. The oath that Saul swore to guarantee her protection must have been a common form of swearing in Israel, but it is ironic that one would swear in this way when he was about to engage in an act expressly forbidden by God.

It is necessary at this point to try to figure out what normally happened during one of these seances with a spiritistic medium. "A woman that hath a familiar spirit" (28:7 KJV), was literally translated, is "a woman in whom there is a divining demon." Saul wanted to find "a woman that has a familiar spirit," or "a woman controlling a divining demon" (v. 7). And he said in verse 8, "Divine [discover or make known] unto me by means of the divining demon the one I shall name." Apparently when a medium went into a trance, he or she communicated not with the dead person but with a demon that impersonated the dead person. The demon then spoke through the medium. It is interesting to note that the Septuagint rendering of the Hebrew 'ob ("one who has a familiar spirit" or "a medium") is eggastrimuthos ("ventriloquist"). So demons might impersonate the dead but could not bring them back.

In this case the usual occult procedure was cut short by the unexpected real appearance of Samuel. The terrified medium "screamed at the top of her voice" (28:12). She saw an apparition that she had not anticipated. Things were not going normally. In some unexplained way she knew that the seeker was Saul and she had been deceived. Saul quieted her fears and asked what she saw. She replied that she saw a "divine" (28:13 NASB), or "spiritual being." He looked like an "old man wearing a robe" (v. 14

NIV). Whether Saul saw Samuel or merely assumed it was the prophet, he immediately prostrated himself in homage. The medium was no longer in control of a demon or controlled by one; after Samuel's appearance, she became irrelevant to the scene. What followed was a conversation between prophet and king.

Samuel asked first for an explanation of Saul's disturbance of him. The king's statement is clear enough; he knew of only one who could intercede for him or reveal to him the will of God. But the reader must wonder how Saul could expect an answer from Samuel if God had forsaken him. Samuel himself made that point (28:16). And, of all things, how could he expect help from a spiritistic medium? Then Samuel pronounced his last judgment on Saul; Saul's day of grace had expired. The kingdom had been torn from him and given to David because of his disobedience. His sin would bring judgment not only on him but also on the nation. Samuel said, "The LORD will . . . give over Israel along with you into the hands of the Philistines" (28:19). The Philistines would thoroughly defeat the army of Israel and thoroughly plunder it for "the LORD will give over the army . . . into the hands of the Philistines." And tomorrow Saul and his sons would be "with me."

Unquestionably this meant that on the next day all of them would be dead—be with Samuel in the abode of the dead. But there is argument over whether this also means presence with Samuel in paradise. There is no reason why Saul should not have gone to the abode of the blessed dead, for he is not portrayed as an unbeliever but a disobedient believer under divine discipline. And Jonathan could not even be viewed as under divine discipline.[1]

Then Saul, who had been kneeling with his head bowed to the ground, sprawled out full length. His system was totally drained. He had been under the strain of a tremendous apprehension that had kept him from eating all that day and night; he had made the difficult journey to Endor; and now he had been given the sentence of death. The medium came to try to revive him with food, saying in effect that she had risked her life to grant his wish and she begged him to grant hers and eat. With great urging, aided by Saul's companions, she finally persuaded Saul to do so. He sat on the bed while she cooked. Then the men ate and returned to the Israelite camp that night. It may be guessed that if Saul returned before daybreak, there was no sleep left in him that night.

12. *David's dismissal from the Philistine army* (29:1–11)

Meanwhile, the reader is filled in on what has been going on behind the Philistine lines. Aphek was serving as a rallying point for their armies.

---

[1]For a further discussion of the subject of Saul and the medium of Endor, see Merrill F. Unger, *Biblical Demonology*, pp. 143–64.

Earlier it had been the site of the main camp when the Philistines defeated the Israelites and took the ark (4:1–11). To this point, about ten miles northeast of Tel Aviv, the "princes" (29:2), or kings of the five Philistine cities, brought the contingents of troops they were contributing to the war effort. David and his men marched along with the troops of Gath; but the "commanders" (29:3), perhaps several subordinate officers or the commanders of the troops under each of the other four Philistine kings, took issue with their presence. Achish explained that since the day David "deserted" (v. 3) to him a year or more before, he had found no fault in him. The wrangle became intense, and the other Philistine leaders would have none of David's participation in the fight. They were plainly afraid that if David changed sides in the middle of the battle, he might turn the tide against the Philistines. Moreover, David's sabotaging the Philistine war effort could restore him to favor with Saul (v. 4).

Having no choice, Achish had to confront David with the decision of the other Philistine leaders. David, possibly suspicious that Achish did not trust him, remonstrated with the king. Achish affirmed once more that he found no fault in David; of course, he did not know the truth of what David had been doing. The rather pious statements "as the LORD lives" (29:6) and "like an angel of God" (v. 9) are not necessarily indications of Achish's softening toward Yahweh or a tampering with the text by some copyist. Rather, these may be courtesy statements or accommodation to David.

The command in 29:10 to leave first thing the next morning, no doubt to avoid further contention, is clear and forthright enough. But it is interesting that in the Septuagint there appears this addition to verse 10: "and entertain no evil thought in your heart" (cf. NEB, JB). The intimation is that Achish feared David would feel insulted and be tempted to take revenge. The next morning David did exactly as he was told, no doubt relieved that an amiable solution had been found to a very thorny problem; he was excused from fighting the Israelites. Evidently the providence of God had been following him again.

13. *Tragedy at Ziklag and Amalekite defeat* (30:1–31)

But it did not seem quite so evident to David that God was with him as he returned to Ziklag. When the Philistines mustered their forces in the northern sector and David pulled all his fighting men out of Ziklag, a power vacuum was created in the south; and the Amalekites took advantage of the situation. Bands of marauders sacked small border towns in southern Judah and Philistia and carried off the entire population of Ziklag and burned the town to the ground (cf. 30:14; Kerethites = Philistines). Presumably the Amalekites were more interested in plunder than mere vengeance, for they did not kill anyone (30:2). It is likely they intended to sell the women and children into the Egyptian slave market.

David and his men arrived "on the third day" (30:1) after leaving Aphek. Since the distance was some seventy-five miles, they had advanced on forced marches about twenty-five miles a day. At the end of the long trek they expected to see their families and to get some rest, but they were greeted by smoldering ruins and a deadly silence. They wept aloud "until there was no strength in them to weep" (30:4 NASB), evidently in a loud lamentation of a ritual kind. David's heartache was both personal and administrative: his two wives and his property were gone, and his men were embittered and talked of stoning him for leaving the place too defenseless.

In the midst of an impossible situation, "David strengthened himself in . . . God" (30:6 NASB); by an act of faith he laid hold on God for comfort and the energy to face the debacle of the moment. Then he sought God's direction as to what he should do next. David's inquiry of God probably was through the offices of Abiathar, who consulted the Urim and Thummim for him. The answer was clear: "Pursue, for you will surely overtake and surely rescue" (30:8) With this unequivocal pledge from God and a prompt and determined command from David, the six hundred went forth to the pursuit with confidence. But the best of intentions cannot push the body beyond the limits of endurance. When the company got to the Besor brook, over ten miles south of Ziklag), about two hundred of them could go no farther; so David ordered them to remain there with the baggage while the rest went on.

Soon, providentially, the troop came on a half-dead young man whom they guessed might be useful to them. They brought him to David, revived him with food and water, and then pumped him for information. He turned out to be an Egyptian slave, who had been owned by an Amalekite involved in the raid on Judean and Philistine territory. In what language the Israelites communicated with him is not clear; they presumably addressed him in their own Canaanite dialect, which he understood sufficiently to respond. A foreign-born slave often was especially expendable in the ancient Near East. If one grew sick or too feeble to be useful any longer, he was frequently left to fend for himself. In this case it was unthinkable that humanitarian concerns should be allowed to impede a military venture, and the young man had been abandoned. Now the Egyptian in a sense owed his life to David's men, and he found it virtually impossible to refuse their request for help in locating the Amalekite marauders.

Perhaps out of revenge he would have been glad to do so. But if he turned informer, he would be at the mercy of both his former owner and his captors. So before he promised to guide them to the Amalekite camp, he exacted an oath that David would not kill him or turn him over to his master after his usefulness was over. "Before God" (30:15 NIV) probably involved Yahweh; the Egyptian would expect David to swear before his own God, and that was good enough for him. There need be no question here of whether the Egyptian was a monotheist or whom he worshiped. Probably the Amalekites were not far away because the Egyptian could not have endured a long journey in his weakened condition; possibly he was provided with a donkey. After David's men caught sight of the Amalekites, the Egyptian is never heard of again. He would make a good subject for a novel about a proselyte to Israel and a faithful member of David's court when he became king of the united kingdom.

When the Israelites came upon the Amalekites at dusk, the latter were carousing with complete abandon—eating, drinking, and dancing—in celebration of their successful plundering ventures. They felt perfectly secure because they thought that all forces posing a threat to them were far away. In fact, they were "scattered everywhere" (30:16), not organized in a tightly knit and defensible camp. Moreover, in their partying they had laid aside their weapons, and many of them must have been drunk or half-drunk. Therefore they were no match for David's forces, who came with a determined zeal to rescue their wives and children. Furthermore, David seemed to have put the entire Amalekite company under the ban and sought to exterminate them. But it was acceptable for David to take booty when Saul could not, because the Israelites were reclaiming what belonged to them.

The whole operation took about twenty-four hours: "from dusk until the evening of the next day" (30:17). When it was over, all the Amalekite raiders were dead except four hundred who escaped on camels. And as was predicted, "David recovered everything the Amalekites had taken. . . . Nothing was missing" (30:18–19). Verse 20 is rather obscure, but the livestock referred to in the first part of the verse must be the plunder taken from other places. It was driven before "the other livestock" (30:20; "the other cattle") that had belonged to the people of Ziklag. The plunder taken was regarded as "David's spoil" (30:20) and was to be distributed as he saw fit.

David's four hundred must have been totally exhausted by the time they finished the action at the Amalekite camp. They had marched for three days, had advanced to the enemy camp the night of the third day, and had engaged in a military action for the following twenty-four hours. They presumably ate at the Amalekite camp and got some sleep before organizing the livestock and their families for the trek northward.

When they arrived back at the brook Besor, there was an ugly altercation between the four hundred, who went to the battle and who did not want to share the spoil, and the two hundred who had stayed behind with the baggage. In dealing with this problem, David first stressed their kinship ("my brothers," (30:23); they were all in this struggle together. Second, he pointed out that God had given the victory; gratitude and justice flowing from it required consideration for those who had guarded

the baggage and thus had performed a necessary function. Then he gave
the judgment that all should share alike, and this statute became a precedent in Israel. Perhaps Numbers 31:27 and Joshua 22:8 helped to formu-
late David's thinking on this occasion.

The concluding verse of chapter 30 chronicles what David did with his
spoil. Some of these places can be identified but others cannot; all were in
Judah, and most of them were in southern Judah. In some cases what was
sent must have been partial indemnity for spoil taken by the Amalekites.
In other instances David merely sent a "gift" (v. 26 NASB) to a town that
had supported him and/or with which he was cultivating good relations.
The fact that there was even a small gift for so many towns shows that
success of the Amalekite freebooting expedition. These gifts paid off in
helping to bring recognition to David as king in Judah soon afterward
when news of the death of Saul came ringing through the land.

B. Saul's Death (31:1–13)

While this drama of death and victory was being acted out in the south,
another of larger proportions was taking place in the north. The dreaded
day of which Samuel had spoken at Endor had arrived. The Philistines
mounted the attack against the Israelite lines in the Valley of Jezreel and
cut them to ribbons with their superior chariotry and archery. Retreating
up the slopes of Mount Gilboa, the Israelites tried to regroup and make a
stand; but the cause seemed hopeless and carnage was great.

Apparently much of the Israelite army simply melted away, but the
sector of the front held by Saul and his sons momentarily stood their
ground and took heavy losses. Saul's three sons were all killed and finally
Saul himself, according to the Septuagint, was wounded "under the ribs"
(literally, "in the hypochondria") by Philistine archers. Unable to fight
any longer, Saul commanded his armorbearer to kill him, lest the enemy
find him alive and "abuse" (31:4 NIV) him—possibly torture him to death.
The armorbearer refused, perhaps out of great respect for the Lord's
anointed. So Saul felt he had no recourse but to commit suicide, not
unfavorably commented on here because soon he would have died anyway. Then the armorbearer also committed suicide because he was ac-
countable for the life of the king. If he were found alive beside the dead
king, he likely would be executed for failure in the line of battle. So Saul,
his armorbearer, three of his sons, and "all his men" (31:6) died on that
day. The latter cannot refer to the whole army and so must apply to his
servants or the bodyguard that stood with him in that sector of the front.

Had David remained a member of the court in good standing, he too
would have perished on that fateful day. By the providence of God he was
totally removed from the theater of action. Saul had one son, Ish-Bosheth,
remaining; for some reason he must not have been at the front. He
possibly had been left at the head of the government in Gibeah. Abner,

commander of the forces, escaped too and later was able to help re-establish the government east of the Jordan (2 Sam. 2:8–10).

When the Israelites heard that Saul and his sons were dead and saw that the resistance had totally collapsed, they became panic stricken. Refugees began to stream out of the villages all along the Valley of Jezreel and the Jordan Valley and fled to the east bank of the Jordan. The Philistines then occupied those towns and thus came to control the whole of northern Israel. Apparently the Israelites continued to maintain a shaky hold on the hill country of Samaria and Judea.

The day after the battle of Gilboa the Philistines plundered the battlefield, making off with jewelry, weapons, and anything else of value. As they did so they came on the bodies of Saul and his sons, evidently identified by clothing, insignia, and seals hung about their necks or in waist pouches. They cut off Saul's head and probably those of his sons and took off their body armor and deposited all of this as trophies in the temple of Ashtoreth, the female deity worshiped beside Dagon. Where that temple was is open to question. Some have concluded it was at Ashkelon, where the most ancient temple of Ashtoreth was supposed to have existed. But a temple of Ashtoreth has been excavated at Beth Shan, and it certainly would have been more convenient to have put the battle trophies there.

The bodies of the four were fastened to the wall of Beth Shan, standing just east of the battlefield and four miles west of the Jordan River. Perched on a dominant hill overlooking the whole region, Beth Shan had walls that could be seen from a considerable distance. The public exposure of bodies of enemy captives was common in the ancient Near East. Meanwhile, messengers were sent throughout Philistia with news of the victory, not only among the people but "in the temple" (31:10). Apparently some sort of memorial inscription was placed in the temples of the five major Philistine cities as a votive offering of thanks to the gods.

As some of the refugees passed Beth Shan and saw the bodies of Saul and his sons, they were horrified but helpless. When they reported it in Jabesh Gilead on the east bank, however, the men of that town felt duty-bound to do something for the benefactor who had rescued them from their plight (11:1–11). They journeyed through the night and stole the bodies of Saul and his sons and brought them back to Jabesh Gilead. Verse 12 states that they "burned" the bodies, according to most translations; but cremation was not practiced in Israel except for an occasional criminal. So it is possible that the bodies were so mutilated and putrified in this case that they were cremated; or possibly by this means further indignities could be prevented. In any case a memorial grave was provided, and a seven-day fast was held in mourning for the honored dead. So ended the pathetic life of one who refused total obedience to God.

For Further Study

1. What principles and practices, developed during David's days of wandering, were to continue during his royal administration?

2. Describe the tight spots from which David was rescued during his days of wandering; note the means by which he was rescued in each case.

3. Tabulate the further steps in the decline of Saul during David's wanderings.

4. Note the responses or reactions of individuals or groups to David in 1 Samuel 21–30.

5. Collect all hints or indications of how David supported himself and his men during his wanderings.

Chapter 5

The Early Years of David's Reign
(2 Samuel 1:1–7:29)

A. David as King at Hebron (1:1–5:5)

1. *News of Saul's death* (1:1–16)

David had waited a long time to take the reins of government. Even though he had been anointed king sometime earlier, and Jonathan and Saul and many others believed he would become king, he often must have despaired of ever holding the office. Of course, he could not take the throne as long as Saul occupied it. The reader has learned that Saul was now out of the picture, but David did not know this. Now the news reaches him. The way he received it and his reaction to it tell much about the character of the man. David clearly had the patience to wait for God to work out His plan for his life in His own way. He was not motivated by personal ambition to the extent that he sought to take developments into his own hands. Above all, he had profound respect for God's anointed sovereign and refused to take the life of one who ruled by divine sanction.

Evidently David's foray against the Amalekites took place about the same time as the battle on Mount Gilboa, because "on the third day" (v. 1) after he returned from retrieving the plunder from the Amalekites, the messenger arrived from Saul's camp. It would have taken him about three days to travel the ninety to one hundred miles from the front. That David could live in ruined Ziklag probably resulted from the fact that ancient Palestinian houses normally had stone or mud-brick walls; so fires started by the Amalekites would not have destroyed everything.

The story of the Amalekite's report is told in minute detail, indicating that it was taken from an original source. Textual critics often allege that an editor used two different accounts of the death of Saul (1 Sam. 31; Chron. 10:3; and here) and did a clumsy job of handling the detail and reconciling the accounts. A high view of inspiration leads to the conclusion that 1 Samuel (1 Chron.) describes what really happened and that the present narrative was a concoction of the Amalekite told for self-serving purposes. Actually, it is possible to harmonize many details of the two accounts, but the description of Saul's death is different in each. There are at least two particulars that cast real doubt on the validity of the Amalekite's story: the intimation that Saul was alone and unattended by Israelite warriors (vv. 6–7) and that Saul would call on a pagan Amalekite to kill him in order to save himself from the uncircumcised Philistines. Evidently the Amalekite found Saul after he had died but before the Philistines came to strip the dead on the battlefield. He made off with the king's crown and arm band and took them to David with a report that he had killed the king—no doubt hoping for some reward from David.

The Amalekite is described as a son of a "stranger" (v. 13 KJV; Hebrew *ger*), a kind of resident alien in Israel. As such he would have been acquainted with the stress between Saul and David and the anticipation that David would be the next king. He came with his "clothes torn" and "dust on his head" (v. 2), the conventional manner of delivering tragic news (cf. 1 Sam. 4:12–17). He fell to the ground before David "in obeisance" (v. 2), appearing to recognize his kingship. As evidence that Saul and Jonathan were dead, he brought Saul's crown (probably a small metallic cap on a band that encircled the head) and his gold arm band (worn on the upper arm by various Near Eastern kings, especially Assyrians).

David's reaction to the Amalekite's tidings were the opposite of what he expected. Instead of being glad that his antagonist was dead and that he was now in line for the throne, David and his men went into mourning. There was plenty to fill David with grief: his dearest friend Jonathan was gone; the army had been decimated; and Israel had been humiliated before the Philistines. In a sort of ceremonial demonstration of sorrow, they tore their clothes, mourned (literally "beat their breasts"), wept or wailed, and fasted until evening (vv. 11–12).

Then, apparently at the end of the day, David called the Amalekite to account. He had had several hours to decide what he would do. Instead of bestowing the expected reward, David reproached the man for daring to kill "the LORD's anointed," whose person was sacred (cf. 1 Sam. 24:6; 26:9; 11, 16). Then he ordered his execution. The Amalekite had confessed to the crime, causing David to observe, "Your own mouth has testified against you" (v. 16 RSV). The man had brought confirmation of the death of Saul with his possession of the king's crown and arm band. Regicide certainly was a capital offense, and David himself did not want to let anyone think he had had any part, however indirect, in the death of Saul. Lacking any alternative account, David took the man's statement at face value. David had said, "Your blood be on your own head" (v. 16). This meant the man's guilt rested on himself and he deserved to die; otherwise, it would rest on David and could be avenged.

2. David's lament (1:17–27)

The latter part of chapter 1 is one of the most beautiful odes ever written. The Hebrew for "lament" is *qinah*, signifying a funeral dirge or mournful elegy. This passage rivals the best of David's poetry in the Psalms. Many believe it became a national war song and that it was taught under the name of "the Bow." The NASB and NIV translations subscribe to this point of view. The Book of Jashar is mentioned in Joshua 10:13 and in the Septuagint of 1 Kings 8:53 and apparently was a book of war ballads or a history of the wars of Israel. To the assertion that this poem is devoid of religious feeling, it may be replied that David's generosity toward his enemy Saul and his great love for Jonathan are products of divine grace.

Saul and Jonathan are described as the "glory" ("beauty") or "ornament" of Israel slain on the heights. "Publish not the good news" (v. 20, Sept.)—good from the Philistine point of view—in Gath or Ashkelon (chief Philistine cities) because the resultant rejoicing would only bring greater humiliation for Israel. Reference to the "daughters of the Philistines" (v. 20) involves the custom of employing women to celebrate victories by singing and dancing (1 Sam. 18:6). Verse 21 calls on nature to join in the mourning: let the mountains of Gilboa remain in perpetual barrenness as a memorial of the tragedy that occurred there. The shields, instead of protecting the warriors, have been defiled with their blood. They are now cast aside, not oiled in preparation for battle.

The figure in verse 22 is that arrows drink the blood of the enemy and the sword devours their flesh. The bow of Jonathan and the sword of Saul are described as being particularly deadly in the hands of these valiant warriors. Saul and Jonathan shared a common fate, but David also attributed to them speed and strength in battle and the virtues of "loving and kindly" (v. 23). These virtues primarily applied to Jonathan, but they also described Saul in his earlier years; and David was generous in his praise of the king. Formerly, Saul with his victories had brought great spoil to the nation, but now the young women who used to come out and sing and dance over his victories and profit from the spoil must weep (v. 24).

David finally turns to a special lament, saying, "I am in anguish" or "I am in a desperate plight" for Jonathan who is "very dear" (v. 26). In fact, in an effort to describe the deepest earnestness of devoted love, he declared Jonathan's love was "greater than the love of woman."

3. David's move to Hebron (2:1–7)

"After this" (2:1), after news of the death of Saul, David knew that it was safe for him to return to Israelite territory and that the road to kingship was open to him. It was logical for him to entertain thoughts of going into Judah, both because he and his wives had come from that area and because he had been careful to maintain good relations with various towns in Judah. But David wanted to be sure that he was in the will of God; so he sought God's direction for his life. He presumably inquired by means of the Urim and Thummim, which evidently involved a kind of casting of lots to determine yes or no answers. First he learned that it was all right to go into Judah. Then he inquired about where he should settle. He presumably submitted names of towns for yes or no answers and it is possible he suggested Hebron first because it was the logical political and geographical center of the region. At any rate he got his direction to go there.

The KJV, following the Hebrew, reads that the company went to the "cities of Hebron" (2:3), referring, no doubt, to the villages near Hebron and belonging to it. David's six hundred men and their families (probably at least fifteen hundred people) and livestock would have inundated the town of Hebron itself; and it seems unwise to change the reading to "city of Hebron" as some versions do. Hebron, with its altitude of three thousand forty feet, it the highest town in Palestine. Nineteen miles southwest of Jerusalem, it stands on the main route from Jerusalem to Beersheba.

Then the "men of Judah" (2:4), representative elders, invited David to be king over their tribe, and he accepted. The actual anointing (2:4) probably would have been done by Abiathar the priest. A public ceremony of this sort was to be expected because Samuel's earlier anointing had been private, and it was not clear how many had any knowledge or understanding of its significance.

Soon after taking the throne, David heard of the bravery of the men of Jabesh Gilead in rescuing the bodies of Saul and Jonathan (1 Sam. 31:11–13) and sent a message of gratitude for their kindness. But the message was at least partly political. David promised to show them "the same favor" (2:6 NIV) as God would and perhaps as Saul had done. Then he exhorted them to continue to display military valor and took the opportunity to inform them of his accession to kingship in Judah. No doubt David meant to imply that it would now be appropriate to transfer to him the great loyalty they had demonstrated toward Saul.

More than likely the Philistines saw no immediate threat in David's rise to leadership in Judah. They presumably continued to regard him as a vassal chieftain, and he continued to recognize their suzerainty. If so, they could virtually claim control of all Palestine west of the Jordan because there was no military power among the other tribes of Israel able to stand against them at that time.

4. Rivalry with the kingdom of Israel (2:8–3:1)

However, it appears that Abner, commander of Saul's forces, was gradually able to pull together the northern tribes of Israel and push back the Philistines. After five and one-half years of interregnum, Abner felt strong enough to install Saul's remaining son on the throne. This conclusion is reached from the fact that David ruled for seven and one-half years in

Hebron and Ish-Bosheth for two years in Mahanaim. Since David's assumption of power over all Israel occurred at the end of Ish-Bosheth's rule, there must have been an extended period of regrouping when there was no king in Israel (2:10–11). Reluctance to declare David king of all Israel during those years may have been due in part to his association with the Philistines.

When the power of the central government had been somewhat reestablished, Abner took Ish-Bosheth, youngest son of Saul, and made him king in Mahanaim, located east of the Jordan and south of the Jabbok River. Evidently it was not yet safe to maintain the capital in the old Benjamite homeland. Ish-Bosheth's power is said to extend to Gilead (where Mahanaim was), the tribe of Asher in the north, the area of the Valley of Jezreel and the highlands of Ephraim and Benjamin, almost as far south as Jerusalem. Ish-Bosheth's original name was Esh-Baal (1 Chron. 8:33; 9:39), meaning "man of Baal", but it was later changed to Ish-Bosheth ("man of shame") in accordance with the common practice of substituting Bosheth ("shame") wherever Baal appeared in a name.

As the two Israelite kingdoms gradually grew stronger, it seemed inevitable that they would come to blows. A casual reading of verse 12 leads to the conclusion that Abner's expansionist activities were now being geared to the takeover of Judah. But his deployment of troops at Gibeon, six miles northwest of Jerusalem in Benjamite territory, may indicate that David had invaded the territory of Israel and that Abner was engaged in a defensive movement. Or David may have advanced into Benjamite territory in order to attack Abner's staging point before he could launch an attack. In any event the two contestants met at Gibeon (modern el Jib).

When the two armies met by the pool of Gibeon, Abner proposed that a select group engage in single combat, perhaps to prevent full-scale civil war and extensive bloodshed. Joab, who appears here for the first time as the commander of David's forces, agreed to the request. Twelve from each side prepared to engage in the deadly war games, and they fought with such ferocity and courage that all twenty-four died within a very brief time.

Thus nothing was decided by the smaller contest; and a fierce battle broke out between the two armies, with David's men putting Abner's to flight. Instead of describing the larger struggle, the historian concentrated on an episode involving Abner, for repercussions of it ultimately would lead to the termination of the northern kingdom. In the army of David were three brothers, sons of David's sister Zeruiah (1 Chron. 2:16): Joab, Abishai, and Asahel. The first was commander of David's forces; the second, a heroic leader of the thirty mighty warriors (cf. 2 Sam. 23:18); and the third, a member of that group (2 Sam. 23:24).

Asahel is singled out as being fleet of foot, like a gazelle (2:18) He pursued Abner, perhaps with the hope of another significant victory and the addition of another suit of armor to his collection of trophies. At least that is the intimation of verse 21. Evidently aware of his physical superiority and the likelihood that he would kill Asahel if they engaged in hand-to-hand conflict, Abner begged him to attack one of the young men with whom he was more evenly matched. Clearly, Abner was not so much motivated by a desire to spare Asahel as he was to avoid the threat of blood revenge by such a formidable foe as Joab (2:22). But Asahel refused to turn aside; so in self-defense Abner was forced to act. He swung backward at him with the butt of his spear, which was sharpened for the purpose of sticking it in the ground. Ramming Asahel through the abdomen, he killed him with one thrust. As Asahel's comrades viewed his corpse, they were so stunned that they simply stopped and looked at him.

Finally Abner was able to pull together his fleeing force and regroup on the top of a hill. Then he called out to Joab to remind him of the bitterness of civil war and begged him to stop the pursuit and end the bloodshed. Joab threw the blame on Abner for the fight because the latter had instigated the single combat. Then Joab acceded to Abner's request and blew the "ram's horn" (2:28) to signal an end to the pursuit. In an effort to put as much distance as possible between his forces and those of Joab, Abner marched all night long back toward Mahanaim. The possibility existed that Joab might renew the conflict when he saw the extent of the advantage he possessed and when he fell to brooding over the death of his brother. He might even order a massive assault as a measure of blood revenge. The magnitude of Abner's defeat is presented with stark statistics: he lost three hundred sixty men to Joab's twenty. Joab's men also marched all night and at daybreak reached Hebron, about twenty-five miles away. On the way they deposited the body of Asahel in his family sepulcher at Bethlehem.

Lest the reader be misled into thinking that this was the end of the conflict between the two kingdoms, the sacred historian states that there was a protracted war between them. In the process the star of David rose while that of Ish-Bosheth set. Though the kingdom of Judah was smaller, it was more of a patriotic unity. The kingdom of Ish-Bosheth consisted of the rest of the tribes—mutually jealous of each other, or at least not very cooperative. Presumably, too, the Philistines continued to harass the north but left David alone. Furthermore, David evidently had much more charisma for leadership than Ish-Bosheth. And, of course, the blessing of God was on David, hastening the day when he would rule over a united Israel.

5. *Rise of David and decline of the house of Saul* (3:2–39)

a. *Growth of the house of David* (3:2–5)

Illustrative of the truth of 3:1, the writer proceeds to narrate the increase of David's family and disaffection in the court of Ish-Bosheth. As with other Oriental monarchs, David soon assembled a harem, and a numerous progeny followed. Six sons were born in Hebron of six different wives. The first two wives came to Hebron with David. He married the other four while at Hebron. The third was the daughter of the king of Geshur, a region of Syria northeast of Bashan. Evidently the marriage was for political reasons and was designed to strengthen David's hand in the north against the kingdom of Ish-Bosheth. The result was disastrous, for Absalom, born of that union, was to lead a rebellion against his father that almost proved to be successful. The practice of making marriage alliances with pagan rulers became common during Solomon's reign and resulted in considerable dilution of Yahweh worship at court and eventually among the populace. Of the last three of David's wives nothing is known. A similar list of David's sons appears in 1 Chronicles 3:1-4. There his second son is called Daniel and here Kileab; so he probably had two names.

  b. *Abner's disaffection and assassination* (3:6-39)

After the death of Saul, Abner "made himself strong for the house of Saul" (3:6 KJV). This indicates that he vigorously supported the interests of Saul's dynasty. Actually, however, the situation was quite different; the NIV gives a preferred reading for 2:6: "Abner had been strengthening his own position in the house of Saul." In other words Ish-Bosheth was a virtual puppet in the hands of Abner. This could easily be concluded from the fact that Abner had pulled the kingdom together after the death of Saul and had elevated Ish-Bosheth to the throne to give legitimacy to his own rule in the kingdom. In this strengthening of his position, Abner finally felt secure enough to appropriate one of Saul's concubines. Such an act was considered to be an act of treason, as virtual pretension to the crown, for the wives of a previous king were the exclusive property of his successor (cf. Absalom's action in 2 Sam. 16:22 and Adonijah's request in 1 Kings 2:17-25).

When Ish-Bosheth rebuked him for his action, Abner flew into a rage. He did not justify his action but merely stated his merits: if he were a despicable "dog's head" (3:8; i.e., of worthless character), he would not have supported the cause of the house of Saul for so long. The breach between Abner and Ish-Bosheth was complete; Abner now swore to turn over the kingdom to David. Abner's statement is somewhat curious, for he not only withdrew support from Ish-Bosheth and totally reversed his policy, but also cloaked his proposed action in pious verbiage that leaves some questions about his course of action. If he knew that God had sworn to give the whole kingdom to David, then how did he dare to frustrate God's plan for so long in maintaining the separate kingdom for Ish-Bosheth? And how did he dare to feed his own greed for power in opposition to God's purposes? At any rate he now determined to translate the kingdom to David and to negotiate with him in such a way as to advance his own interests. Dan and Beersheba, the traditional north-south boundaries of Israel, were about one hundred fifty miles apart. After Abner's haughty and overbearing treatment of his nephew, Ish-Bosheth could say nothing because he was powerless before Abner.

Having determined his course of action, Abner promptly proceeded to execute it. Not knowing how David would respond, he first sent messengers on his behalf. They were instructed to begin by raising a question that indirectly offered their fealty. "Whose land is this?" (3:12) is interpreted to mean, "To whom does it belong except to you?" It was his by God's promise. Then they were to suggest an "agreement" (3:12), which undoubtedly would be mutually beneficial, bringing to David kingship over the north and to Abner personal advantages and immunities.

Before David was willing to receive Abner in person to negotiate with him, he demanded the return of Saul's daughter Michal, who had been given to Paltiel (3:13; cf. 1 Sam. 25:44). It may be argued that David's love for her had prompted the request, but far more was at stake. On political grounds she was important to him (1) to show that he harbored no ill will toward the fallen king, (2) to demonstrate that as son-in-law he was Saul's legitimate successor, (3) the win to himself by this means whatever lingering affection there was for Saul (a child born to the union would join the two rival lines), and (4) to enlist the support of the Benjamites.

Apparently after Abner acceded to David's demand, David felt free to present his request directly to Ish-Bosheth, who was helpless to resist without the backing of Abner. David pointed out that he had rightfully acquired Michal by paying the brideprice; so he could demand her back again with perfect justice (3:14). The king then apparently sent Abner to take Michal from her husband and deliver her to David as the price for admission to David's presence. Michal's feelings are not recorded; but her heartbroken husband followed her, weeping all the way to Bahurim, a few miles northeast of Jerusalem at the border of the kingdom of Judah. There Abner forced him to return home.

Then, before Abner even met David, he carried out negotiations with the elders of the various tribes of Israel in an effort to persuade them to declare for David. In addition, he had private conversations with the leaders of the tribe of Benjamin, which would lose some of its special advantages when the royal family no longer came from its midst. The fact that Abner was at the moment escorting Saul's daughter to a reunion with David may have strengthened Abner's case with the Benjamites. From the way Abner spoke to the elders, the general populace of the northern tribes had decided for David long before (cf. 1 Chron. 12). The promise of Yahweh to which Abner referred (3:18) appears nowhere in Scripture. So he must have had in mind some word of a prophet then in circulation or the general success of David against his enemies as a form of declaration that Yahweh was with him.

Abner was a good example of the hypocritical person who covers his real personal or political motivation with a religious veneer in order to persuade people to think well of him and to enable him to gain his own ends. Actually, he was motivated by malice toward Ish-Bosheth and a desire to ingratiate himself with David and gain a powerful position in the united kingdom about to be set up.

After Abner had won over to David the leaders of all the tribes of Israel, he went to Hebron with twenty representatives of all Israel to confirm Abner's announcement of the intentions of all the tribes. David then hosted a banquet for his guests, after which Abner declared his resolve to convoke a solemn assembly of representatives of all the tribes. These were to enter into negotiations and a covenant with David to the end that he might "rule over all that [his] heart desires" (3:21), i.e., all Israel. Then Abner "went in peace"; he was no longer treated as an enemy, for he had ceased all animosity to David. The text does not say, however, that David "sent him away in peace," as if he guaranteed him some sort of safe conduct. Thus the text prepares the way for the narrative that follows.

David's willingness to negotiate with Abner does not violate his principle of refusing to slay the Lord's anointed. Evidently he considered Abner's overtures as part of God's plan for bringing the kingdom to him. He certainly had no scheme for assassinating Ish-Bosheth and probably did not envision how the king was to be disposed of. David's refusal to condone regicide is forcefully underscored by his treatment of Ish-Bosheth's murderers (1 Sam. 4:12).

As long as there was a Joab, Abner was doomed. As Joab returned from a raid, perhaps against the Philistines or the territory of Ish-Bosheth, he learned with dismay of the hospitable reception accorded Abner at Hebron. Joab apparently conjured up all sorts of bogies. Abner was a man of great military prowess, popular throughout the kingdom, and a successful politician. If he ingratiated himself with David, he would present a formidable obstacle to the ambitions of Joab. So fear, jealousy, and a desire for blood revenge motivated Joab in dealing with Abner. First he tried to cast suspicion on Abner as a traitor (3:25), but David seemingly did not buy Joab's line.

Then Joab decided to act on his own. Evidently in the name of David but absolutely without his knowledge, Joab summoned Abner to return to Hebron for further consultations. Then Joab took him aside in the gate, probably in one of the guardrooms, as if to conduct private negotiations, and slew him there. Joab's brother Abishai was party to the murder, which was carried out in revenge for the death of Asahel in the battle of Gibeon (3:30). What Joab and Abishai did cannot be described as blood revenge in the usual sense of the term because Abner had killed Asahel in battle in self-defense and after repeated warnings.

As David responded to this murder, he found himself in a difficult position. Abner had just brought the northern tribes over to him, and Joab was one of his most powerful supporters in Judah. He confessed that because he had just been anointed king, he was too weak or too new to the position to take the action required in justly punishing a powerful man like Joab (3:39). Therefore he decided to dissociate himself from the crime, to lay a curse on the house of Joab, and leave the retribution to God. David would conduct a proper mourning for Abner, and he would pay public tribute to Abner. And before his death he charged Solomon with the responsibility of executing Joab for the murder of Abner and Amasa (1 Kings 2:5).

First David declared his innocence of the murder and then leveled a curse against the line of Joab. God was called on to avenge the murder of Abner on Joab and his family by punishing them with loathsome diseases (those that bring defilement), physical crippling or inability to perform manly occupations, violent death, and poverty. Next he appointed a public mourning for Abner in which Joab, his courtiers, and his warriors were ordered to participate. This included tearing their clothes, putting on sackcloth (an outer garment of coarse haircloth), and noisy lament. In the funeral procession Abner and David's courtiers and warriors were to precede Abner's bier and David himself followed it.

As part of the mourning David refused food all that day and carried on a public weeping at the grave of Abner in Hebron. Moreover, he composed a funeral ode that in effect said Abner had died a death he did not deserve; he was no common criminal bound in chains but was treacherously murdered. And subsequently he paid tribute to the good qualities of Abner, calling him "a prince" and "a great man" (3:38). The genuineness of David's sorrow for Abner, his tribute to him, and his discreet conduct pleased the people and convinced them of his lack of complicity in the murder (3:37).

6. *Murder of Ish-Bosheth and punishment of his murderers* (4:1–12)

After the death of Abner, the government and public order rapidly disintegrated in the northern kingdom. Ish-Bosheth's "hands went limp" (4:1); he lost the ability to function. Abner had been the mainstay of the king and the chief administrator of the state. The people were "dismayed" or "confounded"—they were at a loss to know what to do.

When foundations are crumbling, there are always individuals who try to take advantage of the situation for personal gain. Two brothers, Baanah and Recab, Benjamites from Beeroth (el Bireh, nine miles north of Jerusalem), were commanders of squadrons in the army; and they hatched a plot to assassinate the king. Negotiations were already under way to deliver the kingdom to David; so they decided to kill the king and claim a reward from David. Parenthetically, the point is made that there was no other viable claimant to the throne (4:4). At this time Mephibosheth,

Jonathan's son, was crippled and only twelve years old (five years old at the death of Jonathan, and seven additional years had passed during David's rule at Hebron).

The two assassins were successful because they came at siesta time, between 12:00 and 4:00, when the king was sleeping and security was extremely lax. Their ruse to gain entrance to the modest palace of Ish-Bosheth was to get wheat (the regular rations) for their companies of soldiers. The Septuagint further explains that the portress at the gate, who had been winnowing wheat, fell asleep; so the pair was able to escape unnoticed after their dastardly deed.

Taking the head of Ish-Bosheth with them as proof of his death, the assassins went from Mahanaim to Hebron by way of the Arabah (Valley of the Jordan) during the night. They announced to David the death of Ish-Bosheth, using the providence of God as a cloak for their villainy. His response was quite different from what they expected. He first made it clear that God saves and takes vengeance (4:9); he did not feel it was necessary to commit crimes to get rid of his enemies. Then he referred to precedent in describing what he had done to the Amalekite who claimed to have killed Saul after he had been wounded. But, as a climax, "much more" (4:11) do wicked men who plot against an innocent and defenseless man on his bed deserve capital punishment. Ish-Bosheth was "innocent" of crime in the assumption of regal power after the death of Saul; in the confused times Abner had forced kingship on Ish-Bosheth, who was a son of the deceased king.

Then David ordered the execution of the two criminals, who by their own confession were guilty of regicide. As was common in the case of criminals guilty of treason, their hands and feet were cut off. Then their mutilated corpses were hanged over the pool in Hebron, a place where there was considerable public activity, as a warning and deterrent to others. Finally, a proper respect was accorded the head of Ish-Bosheth by burying it in the tomb of Abner, his kinsman. Thus David not only showed his abhorrence for such a crime, but also demonstrated that he had no part in this murder.

7. David's acceptance by all the tribes (5:1-5)

With the assassination of Ish-Bosheth, the way was open for David's acceptance by all the tribes. Evidently in response to the efforts of Abner, representatives of all the tribes gathered at Hebron to make David king. They gave three reasons for offering him their fealty. (1) They were his blood relatives; all were descendants of Jacob. Though for a while they may have had some fears of his being a naturalized Philistine, his tenure of rule in Hebron had erased their apprehensions. (2) They recognized his prowess as a military leader and bringer of victory (cf. 1 Sam. 18:5-7). (3) Yahweh had called him to be their shepherd and prince. As noted above (3:9, see comment), Abner had made the same assertion, though no precise previous statement to this effect appears in Scripture. Shepherd became a technical term for a ruler in Israel (cf. Jer. 3:15; Ezek. 34:2–3). The ruler was also known as shepherd elsewhere in the ancient Near East (e.g., Hammurabi in Babylon and the Middle Kingdom pharaohs in Egypt).

Probably after considerable negotiations between David and the elders, they made an "agreement" (5:3), or "compact" (NIV). This certainly involved a recognition of the general rights and duties of kingship (see comments on 1 Sam. 10:25). But in addition it must have included an understanding that the other tribes would enjoy equal rights with the tribe of Judah in the new national monarchy. The conclave lasted three days (1 Chron. 12:39) and involved the presence of numerous military personnel along with the clan leaders.

Though there was hard bargaining behind the scenes, a gala atmosphere prevailed with much feasting and joy in the camp (1 Chron. 12:39–40). A new day was dawning for Israel. Hopes ran high with the installation of a new divinely approved leader who was a proven success on the battlefield. Gone were the days of ineffective leadership and division. The "compact" guaranteed a form of constitutional monarchy; and the fact that David found it necessary to "consult" with every captain of a thousand or a hundred in the army (cf. 1 Chron. 13:1) demonstrated the necessity of ruling by persuasion and personal prowess.

Then "they anointed David king" (5:3). Abiathar probably administered the sacred rites. This was the third anointing of David, the first having been privately performed by Samuel and the second having occurred at Hebron. The chronological note is added that David was thirty when he began to reign and that he reigned a total of forty years: seven and one-half in Hebron and thirty-three in Jerusalem.

B. David's Consolidation of the Kingdom (5:6–6:23)

1. *David at Jerusalem* (5:6–16)

Soon after David's accession as king, he began the consolidation of the kingdom. One of the remaining Canaanite strongholds in the south central part of the land was the strategically located citadel of Jerusalem. Much of the town had fallen to the Israelites during the period of the judges (Judg. 1:8), but the stronghold remained in alien hands. It was especially impregnable because it was surrounded on three sides by deep ravines. In fact, it was so impregnable that the Jebusite defenders believed even the "blind and lame" could ward off attackers (5:6).

But David was determined to take it. He declared that whoever took it would have to use what in Hebrew is called the *tsinnor* (5:8). How that word should be translated has occasioned considerable debate. The KJV reads "gutter," the RSV and NIV have "water shaft," the NEB, "grappling-iron," and the NASB, "water tunnel." It is impossible to be dogmatic on the subject, but there are two main views as to what was involved: (1) that it was necessary to mount a daring attack on a section of the wall by means of grappling hooks; (2) that the Israelites discovered the main water system of the city and scaled that to come up inside the walls and surprise the defenders.

The latter commonly is related to Warren's Shaft, named for Captain Charles Warren, who discovered it in 1867 while exploring underground Jerusalem. This ancient water channel consisted of an upper section that cut diagonally from inside the city wall to a fifty-two foot vertical shaft down which a bucket could be lowered to obtain water from the gushing Gihon spring below. This water system was finally cleared in 1980. It is virtually impossible to scale this vertical shaft; but, according to this view, David promised that whoever should do so and capture the city would become commander-in-chief of the forces (1 Chron. 11:6).

Whatever the *tsinnor* was, Joab managed to conquer the fortress of Zion and claim the reward for his feat. David took up residence there "and called it David's city" (5:9). This, then, was the Mount Zion of biblical times (the hill Ophel, the southeastern hill), known by archaeological investigation to have had about eleven acres inside the walls in David's day. It is not to be confused with the modern hill of Zion, the southwestern hill of the city. Jerusalem was a wise choice for a capital because it was strategically located both geographically and politically (on the border between Judah and Benjamin and the northern tribes).

Verses 9–16 provide a summary statement about a few of David's activities in Jerusalem. He engaged in building projects. The term "Millo" (v. 9) means "filling" and could be an artificial terrace or a tower; in this case it probably was a fortress incorporated into the city wall. Sometime later, evidently in the latter part of his reign, David made a treaty of friendship with Hiram, king of Tyre. By its terms David obtained the coveted cedars of Lebanon and craftsmen for construction of a palace; what he gave in return is not indicated. This relationship with Hiram continued on into the reign of Solomon when Hiram helped to build the temple, a merchant marine and a port, and a palace for Solomon. Hiram's reign of thirty-four years overlapped approximately the last fourteen of David's reign and the first twenty of Solomon's. The topical rather than chronological treatment of this passage should not mislead one to think that Hiram was involved with David early in the latter's reign. Hiram presumably would have made a treaty with David after the Hebrew monarch had become great and it obviously would be advantageous for him to do so.

Contrary to the law, which forbade the king to multiply wives to himself (Deut. 17:17), David also married additional wives in Jerusalem, perhaps some for political reasons. These unnamed women bore him sons and daughters, of whom eleven sons are named. Solomon is the only one of the group who appears again in Scripture, except in parallel passages. Finally, David perceived that Yahweh had established his royal power and that his kingdom was related to God's election of Israel (5:12).

2. *David's victories over the Philistines* (5:17–25)

Soon after David was anointed king, the Philistines became alarmed at the threat a united Israel posed for them, especially when headed by a ruler with such prowess on the battlefield. As long as there were two quarrelsome Israelite states contending for the mastery, and as long as David could be considered a Philistine vassal, the Philistines had nothing to fear. Now they decided to attack before David could consolidate his power and become a more formidable foe. David had probably already left Hebron in preparation for the attack on Jerusalem, and so the Philistines searched him out. Without a fortress in which to protect himself, he "went down to the stronghold" (5:17), some place in the mountain fastness of Judea, perhaps Adullam. The Philistines camped in the Valley of Rephaim, the western approach to Jerusalem.

As a devout servant of Yahweh, David inquired, probably by the Urim, whether he should go into battle and whether God would give him the victory. When assured of success, he went forth to battle and defeated the Philistines at a place near the Valley of Rephaim called Baal Perazim. The place name, meaning "Lord of breaking forth," derived from David's observation that God had broken his enemies as floodwaters break forth and carry away whatever is before them. When the Philistines fled from the battlefield, they left behind their idols. They evidently looked to these for support in the way the Israelites had sought the help of Yahweh when they took the ark into battle against the Philistines (1 Sam. 4). David and his men carried off the idols and burned them (1 Chron. 14:12) as prescribed in the law (Deut. 7:5, 25).

David probably did not have the resources to follow up his victory over the Philistines and thus to reduce them to the point that they could not attack again. So, either later in the year or during the next fighting season, the Philistines gathered in the Valley of Rephaim again. This time when David waited on the Lord for instructions, he was told to circle around behind the enemy and attack them in front of a grove of trees that are variously described in the translations of the Old Testament. A variety of balsam may be intended by the rare Hebrew word. Then David was instructed to wait until he heard the sound of "marching" (5:24) in the tops of the trees as if an army of God was approaching to smite the Philistine camp. When this sound brought panic to the Philistines, David was to advance from the rear.

Following God's instructions, David attacked with tremendous success.

He routed the enemy and destroyed their forces all the way from Gibeon, six miles northwest of Jerusalem, to Gezer, some fifteen miles farther to the northwest. Thereafter the Philistines were contained within their own borders; however, David did not utterly crush them the way he did other peoples surrounding Israel.

3. Bringing the ark to Jerusalem (6:1–23)

After making Jerusalem the capital of his kingdom, David, as a man after God's own heart, sought to rehabilitate the national religion and to establish it properly at the center of national affairs. His efforts especially involved bringing the ark to Jerusalem. To give the occasion proper grandeur, David assembled thirty thousand chosen representatives of the nation to accompany the ark. As the word "again" (6:1) indicates, this was the second general assembly of his reign, the first having occurred at Hebron when he was made king over the united nation. On the appointed day the vast throng marched out of Jerusalem westward to Baale Judah (an alternate name for Kiriath Jearim), about ten miles away. There the ark had rested in the house of Abinadab ever since it had returned from Philistine territory some seventy years before. At this point his "sons" (probably grandsons; Semitic usage sometimes understands the word in the sense of descendant) were custodians of the ark, above which Yahweh revealed His divine presence (2 Sam. 6:2).

Evidently, during the ark's long tenure in the household of Abinadab, little effort had been made to learn the sacred regulations concerning it. Thus neither Uzzah and Ahio nor David and his advisers paid attention to the Levitical laws governing its transportation: for example, it was to be properly covered and carried by Levites and was never to be touched except by staves on pain of death (cf. Num. 4:5, 15, 19–20). So, contrary to divine instructions, they carried the ark on a new cart; and when Uzzah put his hand on it to steady it at the threshing floor of Nacon (place unknown, but certainly near Jerusalem), God struck him down "for his irreverence" (6:7 NASB).

Suddenly the great celebration of David and the other Israelites turned to stunned silence. The "anger" (6:7) that God had demonstrated over the act of Uzzah was reciprocated by the anger of David, but against whom is not clear. Some commentators feel that he was extremely displeased with himself for being a party to faulty arrangements. He could also have been very distraught because what had begun as such an auspicious occasion had turned into a fiasco, and the tragedy was a reflection on his own administration. The name of the place came to be known as Perez Uzzah (meaning "breaking forth upon Uzzah"). Soon David's displeasure turned to the fear of God, the fear of further judgment of God against him and his people. To avoid that and to wait for further light and direction, he decided not to bring the ark into the citadel.

To David and the modern reader, at first blush God's action on this occasion seems to be extremely severe. But what was really at stake was reverence for God and a proper recognition of His holiness. The majesty of God was symbolized by the ark. For decades it had been neglected by the nation. Even its keepers knew or cared little about its proper handling and demonstrated a careless familiarity with divine things.

It is evident that at strategic moments in both the history of Israel and the Christian church, God has deemed it necessary to act in judgment to impress His people with a proper reverence for God and His holiness. For example, He came down in judgment at the foot of Mount Sinai as punishment for idolatry when the Ten Commandments were given. As the Israelites entered Canaan, Achan was judged for his disobedience. In the earliest days of the church He felled Ananias and Saphira in an effort to impress His people with the absolute necessity of purity. And on this occasion when David was calling the nation to a new religious beginning, the same point needed to be made.

The reader is not told how the thirty thousand representatives of the nation responded as they witnessed this act of God, but His fear must have fallen on them also. And the lesson that God sought to teach Israel should not be lost on the present generation with its tendency to ignore the majesty, sovereignty, and holiness of God and the resultant lack of connection between Christian profession and personal holiness.

In a different vein it should be noted that David had a problem of competing sanctuaries as he sought to establish the worship center in Jerusalem. After the massacre at Nob, Abiathar had joined David and had been the channel of divine communication to him. Meanwhile, the tabernacle existed at Gibeon with Zadok, in the line of Eleazar, as priest. And the ark stood at Kiriath Jearim. The bringing of the ark to Jerusalem and its association with the affairs of state would still leave a separate worship center at Gibeon. David presumably was neither strong enough nor willing to go through the trauma of deposing one high priest and combining the competing sanctuaries. Time was in his side. That effort could be made at the death of one of the two strong religious leaders in Israel.

Unwilling to take the ark into Jerusalem, David deposited it in the home of Obed-Edom the Gittite, evidently near the threshing floor where the death of Uzzah had occurred. It is commonly thought that he was called a Gittite because he came from the Levitical city of Gath Rimmon. But it is clear he was a Korahite (1 Chron. 26:1–4). Since the Korahites had carried the ark through the wilderness, it was fitting that the ark should once more be under the care of a member of that tribe. The name Obed-Edom means "servant of Edom" and may indicate servitude to the Edomites at some time. Apparently Obed-Edom fulfilled the Levitical requirements for caring for the ark, and God blessed him and his household.

Weeks passed. There was no evidence that Obed-Edom's household would suffer harm or inconvenience from the presence of the ark. In fact, the ark proved to be a positive good. Meanwhile, David also learned that the reason for God's judgment against Uzzah had been improper transportation of the ark (1 Chron. 15:13). When these two facts converged in David's mind, he resolved to bring the ark into Jerusalem and install it in the tent he had prepared for it.

This time proper arrangements were made for carrying the ark, and extensive preparations were made to ensure that everything would be just right. Then with solemn rejoicing the multitude brought the ark to Jerusalem (1 Chron. 15). But when the bearers of the ark had carried it six paces and saw that God was pleased with their conduct, they stopped and David offered sacrifices. Then the procession continued to the place in the citadel of Jerusalem that David had prepared for the ark. When it was properly installed, David sacrificed burnt offerings and peace offerings; the latter were followed by a fellowship meal for the assembled throng to which David distributed food (2 Sam. 6:19).

When the sacred celebration was over, the people all went home; and David went to the palace to face Michal. David had been clothed in an ephod (probably a short sleeveless tunic) as an undergarment and an outer robe of linen (2 Sam. 6:14; 1 Chron. 15:27). During the procession to Jerusalem, he had been caught up in religious ecstasy and engaged in "leaping and dancing" (2 Sam. 6:16). This had necessitated his "disrobing" (v. 20), which may have been a little undignified but not immodest, for he was still quite adequately covered by the linen ephod. Michal had seen David carrying on from a window and "despised him in her heart" (v. 16).

When he returned home, she greeted him sarcastically for his conduct, especially for "disrobing," as an "empty-headed" or vulgar person does (v. 20). Exactly why Michal was so upset with David is not clear. At the minimum she must have been jealous of maintaining royal dignity, and she must have been insensitive to religious fervor. Justly offended, David retorted, "Before Yahweh I was dancing" (v. 21). He was happy to abase himself before God and to honor Him before the people, and the people would understand his actions. In fact, he would be willing to abase himself even further. Then he reminded her of the fallen fortunes of her family (because of Saul's pride) and God's choice of him instead. The perpetual barrenness of Michal that followed often is considered a result of divine displeasure, but it is perfectly natural to see it as an outcome of the permanent estrangement of David and Michal.

C. The Davidic Covenant (7:1–29)

To the story of the settlement of the ark in Jerusalem, the sacred historian now appends an account of David's desire to build a permanent house for Yahweh. Evidently the arrangement of the text is topical rather than chronological, because David was now "settled in his palace" and had "rest from all his enemies" (7:1). Presumably chapter 7 fits fairly late in David's reign, after most of the campaigns grouped together in the military summary of chapters 8-10.

After David had completed his own magnificent palace with the help of Hiram of Tyre, it seemed incongruous to him that the ark of God should dwell in a tent. His "house of cedar" (7:2) probably was made of limestone and faced on the inside with cedar. As David mused about the construction of a temple for Yahweh, Nathan the prophet gave a personal favorable reaction. Nathan appears on the scene without an introduction, but he was to figure significantly in the biblical narrative: here, in dealing with the sin of David (2 Sam. 12:1-15), and in connection with the succession of Solomon (1 Kings 1:5-48).

That very night God spoke to Nathan, countermanding the personal feelings of the prophet and showing the remarkable difference sometimes made by divine inspiration. God declined David's proposal because up to this time He had lived in a tent among His people, and He had not commanded any tribe or former prince to build Him a house. In fact, the time had not yet come for building the temple. According to Chronicles, God also told David that he was a man of war, and He wanted a man of peace to build the temple (1 Chron. 22:8-10).

Then in grace God turned to David and declared His intent to build a house for His servant David. What He then uttered is known as the Davidic covenant. The elements are these: (1) David would have a son to succeed him and establish his kingdom (7:12). (2) That son (Solomon) would build the temple (v. 13a). (3) The throne of Solomon's kingdom would be established forever (v. 13b). (4) David's house, kingdom, and throne would be established forever (v. 16). (5) Israel would be planted in her own land forever—"not be disturbed again" (v. 10 NASB).

These are unconditional, eternal, and literal promises that follow and enlarge on the unconditional Abrahamic covenant (Gen. 12:1-3; 13:14-17; 15:1-21; cf. Gal. 3:8, 16). To be sure, the Abrahamic and Davidic covenants did not promise uninterrupted occupation of the land or enjoyment of the kingship, but they did pledge that the right to rule would always remain with David's dynasty and that his kingship ultimately would enter an eternal phase. Jesus Christ, in the line of David, was destined to fulfill these everlasting features of the covenants (cf. Luke 1:31-33). One day He will rule on the throne of David on Mount Zion in the messianic kingdom (Ps. 2).

Nathan evidently went to David at the palace in the morning to report all these things God had instructed him to say to the king. Overwhelmed, the busy monarch cleared his appointment calendar and "went in" (7:18), presumably to the shrine of Yahweh, to offer a prayer of praise of God.

Sitting before God in the usual Oriental fashion, on his heels while in a kneeling position and with head erect, he poured out his heart in great humility and thankfulness to God for all His favors. His mind made a rapid recap of all God's wonderful doings on his behalf from his humble beginnings to the present moment: "Who am I . . . that you have brought me this far?" (7:18 NIV) Not only had God watched over him wonderfully to the present, but He had made tremendous promises concerning the distant future. God had done all this "for the sake of your word and according to your own heart" (7:21). The latter refers to the grace and mercy and love that motivate God to perform His works (Exod. 34:6) and the former to some earlier promises that by His very nature He must perform. It is possible that David had in mind the prophecy concerning Judah in Jacob's blessing (cf. Gen. 49:10; 1 Chron. 28:4).

David's meditation on God's goodness to him and his line in the context of the history of Israel led naturally to his reflection on God's care for the nation. God redeemed Israel from Egypt and did mighty things on her behalf, acts that had inspired fear and dread of the glory and power of God. Rehearsal of God's goodness to Israel gave new confidence to David to believe that God would do what He promised to do for him, and he ended with the petition that God would indeed bring His promises to fruition.

For Further Study

1. With the help of a concordance and/or Bible doctrine book, make a study of the holiness of God. What implications does His holiness have for a contemporary Christian lifestyle?

2. Scan the books of Kings to see how the Davidic covenant was fulfilled in the kingship of Judah. Then study the genealogies of Matthew 1 and Luke 3 to see how the Davidic covenant could be fulfilled in Christ.

3. Make a comparative character study of Abner and Joab.

4. Use your imagination a bit. How would the history of the times have been different if Abner had become commander of David's forces?

Chapter 6

David's Conquests and His Sin
(2 Samuel 8:1–12:31)

A. Summary of Conquests (8:1–14)

In the somewhat topical arrangement of 2 Samuel, the author now turns to a summary of David's conquests. It is quite natural for him to begin with the Philistines, because David had tangled with them first after his accession to the throne of the united kingdom. The identification of Metheg Ammah cannot be determined absolutely, but it is probably to be equated with Gath and its villages (cf. 1 Chron. 18:1). Metheg Ammah means "bridle of the mother" (city); if "David took Metheg Ammah [the bridle, Gath] out of the hand of the Philistines" (8:1), he took from them the bridle by which they had kept Israel in check. And it may have been the bridle or control station to keep the Philistine cities in check. The victory was at the same time real and symbolic, militarily effective and symbolic of his breaking the back of Philistine power. But he merely contained the Philistines; he did not occupy their land.

Next the focus of attention shifts southeastward to Moab (8:2). Whatever friendly relations had existed between David and the Moabites (1 Sam. 22:3–4), they had evaporated. After defeating them, David used a well-known tactic for dealing with enemies notorious for their atrocities. He made them all lie down on the ground and passed a measuring line over them, putting to death two-thirds of them (Hebrew text; the Septuagint and Vulgate say one-half). Ancient Jewish commentators state that David's actions were a result of their having massacred his parents and family.

Then the spotlight swings to the north. There David defeated Hadadezer, king of Zobah, located south of Hamath and apparently in the Beka Valley between the Lebanon and Anti-Lebanon ranges. David caught him in a weak moment as he was trying to reassert his sovereignty to the north along the Euphrates River. After a decisive battle near Hamath (1 Chron. 18:3), David captured twenty thousand foot soldiers, seven thousand cavalrymen (according to 1 Chron. 18:4, probably the correct figure) and one thousand chariots (1 Chron. 18:4). David hamstrung or lamed the cavalry and chariot horses and thus made the chariots useless, but he saved enough horses for one hundred chariots. Though chariots had been important to the Hittites and Egyptians centuries before, they were not so widely used in Mesopotamia and (Syria) Aram until somewhat later and were of limited use in hilly Palestine. Solomon kept only fourteen hundred chariots in his armory (1 Kings 10:26).

The region between Palestine and the Euphrates was divided into several small competitive kingdoms. Occasionally some of them joined together when threatened by an outside force. When David trounced the king of Zobah, the Arameans of Damascus became alarmed and swung into action against the rising colossus of the south, but to no avail. Had the Arameans joined forces with Zobah as soon as David came north, the story might have been a little different. David demolished the Damascene army, stationed occupation forces in their chief towns, and put the kingdom to tribute. Thereafter, Toi, king of Hamath, north of Zobah on the Orontes River, sent a delegation to David. Relieved by the removal of his dangerous enemy in Zobah, he apparently sought an alliance with David, or at least his protection. The sending of a high-level delegation headed by his son and rich gifts must have involved more than mere congratulations.

David subsequently engaged in a campaign against the Edomites. The reference in the Hebrew text to Syria or the Arameans in verse 13 is clearly a copyist's error. The parallel passage in 1 Chronicles 18:12, the Septuagint, and 2 Samuel 8:14 all show that the war was against Edom. On this occasion Abishai was military commander (1 Chron. 18:12). The Valley of Salt cannot be identified with certainty but likely was the Arabah south of the Dead Sea. The victory over Edom was complete, and David stationed occupation forces in the key centers of the country.

Now Israel had achieved reasonably secure borders. David had subdued the Edomites, Moabites, and Ammonites on the east of the Jordan (8:12, 14). Thus the foes of Hebrew tribes settled there were dislodged and the tribes were secure. Likewise, the southern frontier was pacified with the defeat of the Amalekites, the western frontier with the subjugation of the Philistines, and the nothern frontier with the vanquishing of Zobah and Damascus. The repetition of the statement "The LORD gave David victory wherever he went" (8:6, 14) helps to underscore divine involvement in the cause of Israel.

David collected tremendous amounts of booty from the various peoples he subjugated. From Zobah he brought the shields of gold carried on ceremonial occasions by courtiers of Hadadezer, as well as a large quantity of bronze. From Hamath came silver, gold, and bronze. And from the other nations he collected silver and gold and other wealth. Down through the ages sovereigns of the East have hoarded quantities of treasure; David did too but with a difference. After meeting his expenses, he dedicated vast

quantities of precious metals to Yahweh for construction of the temple
(8:11). The shields of gold taken from Hadadezer (8:7) found their way into
the temple treasuries and stayed there until carried off by Shishak I of
Egypt during the days of King Rehoboam in 926 B.C. (1 Kings 14:26).

B. Administrative Details (8:15–9:13)

During all of David's foreign wars, he maintained an excellent system of
government at home. In saying David ruled over "all Israel" (8:15), the
historian puts emphasis on the united kingdom. As an ideal king David
maintained "law and justice" (v. 15). In connection with what follows,
with the naming of heads of departments of government, the conclusion
must be reached that David himself acted as chief justice of the court
system and was relatively accessible to the people. Joab was commander
of the army, having gained his position by heroism in the conquest of
Jerusalem (5:8). He maintained this role throughout David's reign until
he supported Solomon's rival for the throne (1 Kings 1–2). Jehoshaphat
acted as "remembrancer" (8:16); as recorder or historian he would have
kept the annals or registered the current events. Zadok and Ahimelech,
the son of Abiathar, are listed as priests (8:17); in the latter case the names
of father and son seem to have been reversed as the result of a copyist's
error. Zadok had been priest under Saul and Abiathar under David; now
both retained their dignity. Seraiah as scribe or secretary of state kept the
records and carried out instructions. Benaiah commanded the royal bodyguard of Kerethites and Pelethites, mercenaries from Philistia. David
followed the practice of many rulers to secure a bodyguard of mercenaries
rather than home guards because they were more dependent on the ruler
alone.

The bureaucracy also included David's sons, who in the Hebrew are
called "priests" (8:18). But evidently they did not perform a priestly function. In the parallel passage in 1 Chronicles 18:17 they are called "the first
at the hand of the king," which the NIV translates as "chief officials at the
king's side." And in 1 Kings 4:5 the priest is called "the king's friend," or
adviser. Justifiably the NIV translates 2 Samuel 8:18, "David's sons were
royal advisers."

A very human and tender aspect of David's administration concerned
fulfillment of his covenant with Jonathan. It is appropriate that the sacred
historian inserted it here because Jonathan had said something about
David's caring for his family when the earth should be rid of David's
enemies (1 Sam. 20:15). David did not know that his friend had any
surviving children (9:1), but members of the court discovered one of
Saul's servants who could provide information on family affairs. This Ziba
was himself a man of considerable substance, judging from his numerous
progeny and servant staff (9:10). Ziba informed David that Jonathan had a
son crippled in both feet. This son, Mephibosheth, was born during

David's wanderings and was dropped by his nurse and crippled at age five during the flight after the disastrous battle of Mount Gilboa (2 Sam. 4:4). Since he had been living in seclusion ever since, David had no knowledge of him. Ziba reported that Mephibosheth (or Merib-Baal, 1 Chron. 8:34), could be found in the household of Makir, a well-to-do landowner of Lo Debar near Mahanaim (9:4; cf. 2 Sam. 17:27–29).

So David summoned Mephibosheth to come to Jerusalem, and he appeared before the king with great trepidation. This may have arisen naturally in one who came to the court of the mighty king from seclusion in a provincial town. But more likely it was generated by the common practice of ancient Near Eastern peoples to exterminate the remaining members of a fallen dynasty.

David gave Mephibosheth his personal assurances of kindness and backed them up in a tangible way with the grant to him of all his grandfather's royal estates. These were now David's by the right of his wife Michal, or they were his by forfeiture to the crown on his accession to power—no other family member being present to claim them. Moreover, Mephibosheth was welcomed to the king's table to dine with his sons as a member of the family. Presumably Mephibosheth would live at home most of the time but would join the king on various public occasions. Such an honor was particularly noteworthy in view of his physical imperfections. Mephibosheth was overwhelmed with kindness. No doubt he had been made to feel that he was a useless member of the family ("a dead dog" 9:8); now he took a new lease on life.

Then to enable Mephibosheth to maintain an establishment suitable to a son of the king, he assigned Ziba and his family and servants to manage Mephibosheth's estates. Some commentators conclude that Ziba already had been supervising these estates for David and now simply changed masters. The size of Ziba's family and servant staff guaranteed Mephibosheth an entourage befitting his status as a son of a king. Presumably Ziba worked the land on some sort of share arrangement, and he committed himself to do as the king had commanded. The mention of Mephibosheth's son Mica (Micah) alerts the reader to the fact that Jonathan's line did not die out but was perpetuated through the descendants of Mica (9:12; cf. 1 Chron. 8:34–40).

C. The Ammonite War (10:1–11:1; 12:26–31)

This war with the Ammonites and their Aramean (Syrian) allies was probably the fiercest that the Israelites had to fight during the reign of David. The conclusion of the war has been noted already in the summary of David's victories (2 Sam. 8:3–8). The struggle now is expanded more in detail, perhaps because of its ferocity, its leading to the Aramean campaign, and its provision of the context for David's sin. The occasion for the conflict appears in 10:1–5; Joab's conflict with Ammon and the Arameans in verses 6–14; David's battle against the Arameans in verses 15–19; the final stages of the conflict under the leadership of Joab and David in 11:1 and 12:26–31.

"In the course of time" (10:1 NIV)—the chronology is indefinite—King Nahash of Ammon died and his son Hanun took the throne. David determined to "show kindness" (10:2) to the son as the father had to him. It does not seem likely that this Nahash was the same one involved in the atrocity story of 1 Samuel 11 because almost forty years of Saul's reign and perhaps fifteen or more of David's had elapsed since that event. Perhaps a second Nahash had ruled after his father, and his kindness to David may have been connected with the rivalry between David and Saul. Moreover, David actually may have had a treaty of friendship and commerce with Nahash as he did with Hiram or Tyre. The NEB translates, "I must keep up the same loyal friendship with Hanun" (10:2). At the minimum David's representatives went to participate in the mourning for the dead king and to extend best wishes to the new one.

Evidently the change of rulers meant a change of policy, and the new king's advisers were able to persuade him that David really intended to spy out the defenses of the capital city (Rabbah or Rabbath-Ammon, modern Amman, about twenty miles east of the Jordan). Accepting their interpretation of David's delegation, Hanun deliberately set about to insult David by humiliating his representatives. He had half their beards cut off, a most disgraceful treatment of an ancient Semite, for whom beards were symbols of status. And he ordered that their long flowing robes be cut off up to their hips, immodestly exposing them. Then he sent them home. When word of their treatment reached David, he sought to save them embarrassment by detaining them at the border town of Jericho until their beards were grown.

This action was tantamount to a declaration of war. And when Hanun saw he had become a "stench in David's nostrils" (10:6 NIV), he scurried around to find allies for the coming fray. He settled on a substantial number of mercenary troops from Aramean states in the north, and that is how these far northern principalities became involved in hostilities with the Israelite state. Beth Rehob probably was located just north of Dan; Zobah has been noted (see on 2 Sam. 8:3); Maacah seems to have stood northeast of the Sea of Galilee; and Tob was southeast of that body of water.

Then David mobilized the army and sent it out under the command of Joab. Apparently Joab walked into a trap that may not even have been planned. Evidently the Ammonites came out of the city and drew up in battle array and Joab deployed his forces before them. Meanwhile, the Aramean mercenary troops were still "in the open field" (10:8), out of sight at his rear. Soon Joab realized that he could easily be squashed in a pincers movement. He determined rightly that the Arameans should be defeated first and probably were more vulnerable because they were hired troops and were without a fortification to fall back on. The Ammonites, on the other hand, were fighting for their homes and had the walled city of Rabbah to protect them.

So Joab divided his forces and prepared to lead the attack against the Arameans, while his brother Abishai faced the Ammonites and held them in check. Then Joab encouraged his brother with a promise of mutual help and issued the exhortation, "Be strong . . . for our people and the cities of our God" (10:12 NIV). The cities of the land belonged to God, who had given the land to the people of Israel. Yahweh's possessions must not be allowed to fall into the hands of the heathen. Joab's attack was completely successful and the Arameans fled. When the Ammonites saw that their support forces had been dissipated, they panicked and fled inside the city walls. Joab probably did not have the resources to lay siege to the city, and/or it may have been too late in the year to begin the siege; so Joab returned to Jerusalem with his army after a successful campaign.

After their defeat the Arameans apparently went back home. Realizing that they would be forced to fight on alone, they pulled together all the troops they could muster. Hadadezer of Zobah called on his vassal states north of the Euphrates to send contingents to the collection center of Helam, south of Damascus and near the border with Israel. Shobach, commander of Hadadezer's army, was to lead the combined force. When David learned of his threatened invasion, he mobilized the armies of Israel and apparently moved with great energy against the Arameans. The last part of verse 17 implies that he surprised the Arameans to a degree and then went on to rout them completely.

The casualty figures present difficulties for the Bible student, however, due both to the general problem of the transcription of numbers in the Old Testament and some copyists' errors in the books of Samuel. The present passage, with its seven hundred charioteers and forty thousand horsemen, is to be compared with 1 Chronicles 19:18, where the number of charioteers is given as seven thousand and the foot soldiers as forty thousand. If this refers to the same conflict as reported in 2 Samuel 8:3–8 (cf. 1 Chron. 18:4–5), then the combined losses reported are forty-two thousand foot soldiers and seven hundred horsemen (seven thousand in 1 Chron.). The armies consisted of cavalry, chariotry, and foot soldiers, and losses were sustained in all three categories; evidently the combined losses in foot soldiers killed and captured were about forty thousand, but it is not possible to be quite so sure about casualties in the other two categories. It is possible that the combined losses in the cavalry and chariotry units stood at seven thousand. Characteristically, no Israelite losses are recorded.

The conclusion to be reached from the two accounts in 2 Samuel and the two in 1 Chronicles is that the Israelites scored tremendous victories against the Arameans, with much heavier losses on the Aramean than on the Israelite side. In fact, the Arameans were so decisively squashed that the vassals broke away from Hadadezer and became subject to Israel; evidently Hadadezer also became tributary to Israel. Moreover, the Arameans were no longer able or willing to help the Ammonites; thus the Israelites were spared a continuing two-front war.

After this fall engagement in the north, the rainy season set in and warfare ceased. The end of the rains signaled the beginning of the campaign season once more, and David sent the armies against the Ammonites under the leadership of Joab (11:1). After initial victories in the countryside, Joab began the siege of the capital city of Rabbah. It was during this siege that David's adultery , the murder of Uriah the Hittite, and the birth and death of Bathsheba's son took place. Thus the siege evidently lasted about a year and involved some fierce contests (e.g., 11:15). It is not necessary to conclude that Solomon was actually born before David joined the men at the front (12:24), thus requiring a two-year siege; it is enough that Bathsheba was "comforted" and had another child on the way before David went to Rabbah.

Joab was finally successful in taking the lower city, the "city of waters" or "waterfort," the area where the water supply was located (12:26–27). With the main source of water gone, the defenders could not hope to hold out much longer. As a loyal subordinate, Joab wanted David to have the honor of taking the citadel; so he urged the king to come with some reinforcements and complete the conquest. David complied and conquered the city, bringing Ammonite resistance to an end.

The booty was entensive; one item that engendered considerable comment was an immense gold crown with an inlaid jewel. This crown weighed a talent, in Israel reckoned to be about seventy-five pounds. In 12:30 the Hebrew word *malkam* could be translated "of their king," but could just as easily be rendered "of Milcom," the chief Ammonite deity (cf. 1 Kings 11:33). A crown that heavy would probably never have been worn by a king but could have been supported by a statue of the god. The crown may have been set on David's head for a moment, but the antecedent of "it" could be the large "precious stone" taken from Milcom's crown and then put in David's crown.

In any case the Ammonite kingdom was brought to an end. Verse 31 sometimes is interpreted to apply to the awful torture frequently imposed on vanquished peoples in ancient times. However, many of the newer interpreters view this as a description of hard labor at such menial tasks as mining, cutting wood, making bricks, and other exhausting occupations.

D. David's Sin (11:2–27)

When the army went off to the Ammonite war, David remained in Jerusalem. This was not necessarily a dereliction of duty, as sometimes is charged, because kings did not always lead their forces into war. In fact, the time came when it was deemed unwise for David to accompany the troops because his personal safety was too important to the state (2 Sam. 18:3). Moreover, the autocratic kings of the ancient Near East had so much administrative detail to attend to at home that they could not always handle both military and domestic affairs adequately. But while David was in Jerusalem he got into trouble. A remarkable feature of Scripture, and certainly one of the indications of its inspiration, is the fact that it does not varnish over the faults of the great leaders of biblical times. No doubt this reporting is intended as a warning to others (1 Cor. 10:11–12).

One day after his siesta, David was walking on the roof of his flat-topped house. It was simple for him to look down into a nearby open courtyard and see a beautiful woman taking a bath. One cannot exactly accuse Bathsheba of inviting trouble, but she was not as modest as she might have been. She must have known that she could be seen from the rooftops of nearby houses. Her conduct gave rise to lustful desire in David, so he immediately inquired about her. He apparently had some prior knowledge of her, because when given some information, literally, "he said to himself, 'Is this not Bathsheba?'" (11:3). That she was married and the wife of one of his outstanding warriors did not stop him. He "took her" (11:4) and had sexual relations with her. Oriental potentates reserved the right to add to their harems, but a man of God was supposed to conduct himself in a different way.

There is no indication that Bathsheba resisted David, and in fact she seems to have been a very ambitious woman. She came to dominate him to a degree and soon secured from him the promise that her son Solomon would take precedence over the other children in the harem and would become the next king (cf. 1 Kings 1:13, 15, 17, 28). As soon as Bathsheba knew she was pregnant, she informed David so he could take steps to protect himself and her (cf. Lev. 20:10).

David's first step was to cover himself by bringing Uriah back from the front to be with his wife; then the pregnancy could be passed off as a normal one within the family. But Uriah did not do what David expected. This naturalized foreigner (a Hittite) developed a magnificent loyalty to Israel's God and a high sense of military duty and propriety. He slept at the door of the king's house with the guards of the king and never went near his wife, even when David got him dead drunk in an effort to break down his inhibitions.

In addition to his high sense of duty, Uriah may have had his suspicions aroused when the king seemed to keep urging him to go home and be with his wife. Moreover, he may have learned from someone that Bathsheba had visited privately with David. Jerusalem was a small place, and it would have been hard to keep a secret for very long. He need not necessarily have been suspicious, however, because David's questions were all about progress at the front; and his being singled out to bring news from Joab was not unusual because he was classified as one of David's "Thirty" heroes (2 Sam. 23:39). In any case the uprightness and piety of Uriah stand in stark contrast to the sinfulness of David.

In order to cover himself and Bathsheba, David seemed to believe he had to dispose of Uriah. In this case it was fairly simple; he could have him killed in battle. So the king sent Uriah's death warrant to Joab by his own hand! The instruction was simple: put Uriah in a dangerous spot on the battle line and retreat from him so he would be killed. Joab loyally followed orders without question, and this privileged information henceforth would give an advantage in dealing with David. In fact, that advantage is evident in this passage, for Joab told the messenger that if David became irritated over the loss of some of his finest soldiers in the foray, he was to inform David that Uriah was dead.

The whole passage reeks with the callousness of David. He ordered the cold-blooded murder of Uriah and sent the orders by Uriah's own hand. He reacted to the death of Uriah and his other gallant soldiers in a very insensitive fashion: "the sword devours one as well as another" (11:25). After an affectation of mourning (the usual period was seven days), he married Bathsheba with consummate haste. But the historian observed: "What David had done was evil in the sight of the LORD" (11:27) and thus prepared the way for the judgment to follow.

E. Judgment on David and His Repentance (12:1–25)

God left David in his unrepentant state for almost a year. In the meantime Bathsheba's son had been born. He finally sent the prophet Nathan to pronounce judgment on the wayward king. As was often the practice in the ancient Near East, Nathan chose to communicate his message by means of a parable. In this case the parable provided an indirect means of pronouncing judgment, and it enlisted David on the side of the prophet before the pronunciation of doom. The story was founded on a common practice of the pastoral people of Palestine to bring up a pet lamb in the family. The reprehensible conduct of the rich man in taking the poor man's ewe lamb while sparing his own flock stirred David's indignation. And as the chief judge of the nation who was supposed to adjudicate justice to the poor and oppressed, he delivered the sentence that the rich man was worthy of death for his crime and that he should restore fourfold, according the law of Moses (Exod. 22:1). For the moment he failed to apply the story to himself; and as is so often true, he clearly saw the fault in another while excusing the same fault in himself (Matt. 7:3–5).

Then, with the fearlessness of a man of God in possession of the truth and under the direct command of God to deliver a message, Nathan addressed himself to his king, who in his absolute authority had the power to strike him dead. With devastating directness, he announced to David,

"You are the man!" (12:7), i.e., you are the one guilty of the heinous injustice portrayed in the parable. God had made David king over Israel from which any number of virgins could have been obtained. God had given David everything that was Saul's, including his wives if he had wanted them. But David had murdered Uriah the Hittite by means of the sword of the heathen Ammonites and had taken his wife to be his own.

Therefore the judgment against him was to be twofold. (1) The sword would never depart from his house, and insurrection would rise against him in his own household. This prophecy was fulfilled in the murder of Amnon (2 Sam. 13:28), Absalom's revolt and death (2 Sam. 18:14), and Adonijah's execution (1 Kings 2:25). His sin certainly weakened his authority and respect with his own family. In addition, because his sins had done great injury to the cause of the true faith, Bathsheba's child would be struck down. If David's punishment was supposed to be fourfold (12:6), it was accomplished in the four deaths in his family. (2) While his sin was committed in secret, his wives would be taken from him and another would violate them in broad daylight and in public. This was fulfilled by the action of Absalom (2 Sam. 16:22).

Nathan's words of judgment pierced the heart of David like an arrow. To his credit, he did not rationalize or offer excuses but bowed before God in true contrition. God graciously forgave his sin and spared his life; the record of David's spiritual experience during this crisis period appears especially in Psalms 32 and 51. But though David was pardoned and restored to divine favor, his reputation was forever besmirched; and the effects of his sin would continue to plague his life and the history of his dynasty for a very long time to come.

Soon after David's encounter with Nathan, Bathsheba's child fell ill. David sought God in prayer, fasted, and lay on the ground. His agony probably rose not merely from his love for the boy but from the chastisement he was enduring. The "elders of his household" (12:17), his older and most trusted servants, were unable to persuade him to get up off the ground and eat. When the child died on the seventh day, they were afraid to tell him. He had been so distraught during his illness that they were afraid David might do something dangerous if he learned of the child's death. When he saw them whispering in little cliques, he guessed the truth. Then he surprised them by getting up, taking a bath, and changing his clothes. He went to the sanctuary to worship and then returned home to eat. This was the reverse of one's usual behavior; normally mourning and fasting followed the death of a dear one.

When his puzzled servants asked David about his actions, he explained that his agonizing before God had been with the hope that God would be gracious and spare the child. But now that the child was dead, such importunate conduct was of no avail; there was no way to bring him back to life. His statement "I shall go to him" (12:23) indicates a belief in immortality and possibly a belief in infant salvation. Certainly, David expected to be in the presence of God in the hereafter; if the two of them were together, both of them would be in the presence of God. Admittedly, however, emphasis here is on the inevitability of death—of David's as well as his son's.

A postscript to this judgment scene is a note about the second pregnancy of Bathsheba and her comforting by a replacement for the son she had lost. The child was named Solomon, meaning "peaceable" or "a man of peace." David probably had in mind a renewal of peace with God; but Solomon's birth may have come at the close of the Ammonite war, at a time when there was hope for an extended period of peace between Israel and her neighbors. That was not the end of the matter, however. Nathan came, apparently on Yahweh's instructions, to name the child Jedediah (meaning "beloved of Yahweh") because "Yahweh loved him" (12:25 JB). When one considers all that has gone before, it is a remarkable act of divine grace that God should show such favor to Solomon and that in His sovereignty He should choose him as the next king of Israel. But then, why did God choose Jacob instead of Esau or David as the youngest of the family? His sovereign ways often are beyond human comprehension.

While God did not spare the great leaders of Scripture from an exposé of their weaknesses and sins, He did not delight in detailing the seamy side of life either. The recounting of the sins of saints of old, and David in this case, had as its purpose the provision of numerous lessons for believers of subsequent ages. (1) David apparently thought he could live like other kings in his disregard for the law of God, but he could not. Just so, other believers are not above God's law and can expect to be judged for their infractions of it. (2) David found that it was foolish to try to cover up sin; by trying to do so he just got deeper into trouble. (3) Sin not only separates a person from God but it also besmirches his reputation and that of God and produces evil effects on other persons, organizations, and institutions. Forgiveness restores the individuals' fellowship with God, but the effects of sin remain. Such a fact should offer a deterrent to the rash acts of believers.

(4) David's capitulation to temptation raises the question of how to avoid such a catastrophe. Two suggestions are especially important. (a) Sometimes by an act of the will one deliberately has to flee a variety of compromising situations. When David saw Bathsheba below, he could have avoided extended observation. Joseph deliberately fled from the presence of Potiphar's wife (Gen. 39:12). The biblical injunction is to "flee from youthful lusts" (2 Tim. 2:22 NASB). (b) One reason why David sinned —the same reason why some modern believers sin—is because of too many idle moments. Even though David was a chief of state, the burden on him was nothing like that placed by a modern complex society on a chief executive. Contemporary individuals often have a job that requires

only forty hours or less of their time. If a person is not careful, there is too much free time for getting into trouble. One way to overcome the problem is to plan purposeful leisure time for oneself and family. Those who are occupied with productive activity, the work of God, and wholesome recreation are not so likely to capitulate to temptation.

For Further Study

1. Make a study of temptation in Scripture, noting reasons why believers are tempted, ways in which they are tempted, and means of overcoming temptation.

2. Draw a map of the area of Palestine and Aram (Syria) and label the parts that David brought within his kingdom.

3. Using a concordance and a Bible dictionary or Bible encyclopedia, trace the genealogy of Jonathan (1 Chron. 8:34–40) to see if any of those men distinguished themselves.

4. Study the biography of Joab to see how he sometimes lorded it over David or got his way, or at least partially disobeyed David's commands. This resulted in part from his involvement in the Uriah affair.

5. With the help of a Bible dictionary, study the history of Rabbah (Rabbath-Ammon). Study also the history and development of modern Amman.

Chapter 7

Absalom's Revolt and David's Restoration to Power
(2 Samuel 13:1–20:26)

The sacred historian wasted no time in reporting the fulfillment of the severe judgment on David. Almost immediately he recorded the sickness and death of Bathsheba's son. In the very next chapter he began the tale of rape and murder and rebellion within the family. In 12:10 Nathan had predicted, "The sword shall never depart from your house"; and in the next verse Yahweh had given notice, "I will raise up evil against you out of your own household." Chapter 13 records the first bloodletting with Absalom's murder of Amnon and the start of the estrangement between Absalom and David.

A. Amnon's Incest and Absalom's Revenge (13:1–39)

As the story opens three individuals are introduced. Absalom and Tamar were David's children by Maacah, daughter of the king of Geshur (2 Sam. 3:3); Amnon was David's son by Ahinoam the Jezreelitess (2 Sam. 3:2). Amnon developed an unholy passion toward his half sister, but he had no opportunity to see her alone because unmarried women in the harem were kept in seclusion ("she was a virgin, and it seemed impossible," 13:2). The children of each mother normally lived in separate quarters. Amnon, the king's eldest son and heir presumptive to the throne, was literally pining away with passion for Tamar. When prodded by his close friend Jonadab, he revealed his problem. Jonadab, a son of David's brother and therefore Amnon's cousin, was a crafty fellow and devised a stratagem to enable Amnon to have an unrestricted conversation with Tamar. Amnon was to feign illness and then ask the king to send Tamar to prepare some fancy cakes for him. All worked out as Jonadab had suggested, and David sent Tamar to perform the desired service for Amnon. Tamar went both because she was ordered to do so and possibly because she felt honored by the invitation.

When Amnon tried to force her, Tamar resisted the best she could. First she begged that he not "dishonor" or "humiliate" her (13:13). Then she appealed to the normal and accepted standards of right conduct in Israel. Next she pointed out that both of them would be ruined by this act. Shame would follow her everywhere; he would be classified as a fool, as one who had no regard for the proprieties of human conduct, as a mere beast (cf. Ps. 73:22). Finally, as a last resort, she urged him to go through proper channels and ask the king for her. There is no indication she wanted that or believed it would happen; it was clearly a delaying tactic. Though the Mosaic Law forbade half-brother and half-sister marriages (Lev. 18:9, 11; 20:17), there is no indication that the law was fully obeyed. A well-known example of this practice before the Mosaic Law was given is the marriage of Abraham and Sarai (Gen. 20:12).

But Amnon would listen to no entreaty, and by brute force he overpowered the ill-fated Tamar. Then, as often happens with persons motivated by violent and base passions, Amnon went from one extreme to another. Seized with a sudden revulsion for Tamar, perhaps because of his guilt and dread of exposure, he ruthlessly drove her from his house. Tamar remonstrated that the wrong done to her in sending her away in this fashion was greater than the wrong already perpetrated, because it would look as if she had been guilty of some shameful conduct, i.e., had initiated the seduction. In fact, his bolting the door behind her as he did made it appear that she was guilty of the sin of initiating the action.

Tamar was dressed in a "robe with long sleeves" (13:18), some sort of rich garment worn by the unmarried princesses (the same term is used for Joseph's special coat, Gen. 37:3). In a stance typical of mourning, she put ashes on her head, tore her garment, and went away wailing the mourner's wail. She put her hand on her head in place of the veil which probably still lay in Amnon's chamber. It was as if she was already dead as a result of the evil committed against her. She was condemned to remain "desolate" (13:21), or childless, in a society where women enjoyed as their greatest crown children to endear themselves to their husbands. When Tamar came running into the house in this fashion, Absalom guessed what had happened. He tried to console his sister and, of course, offered his full protection. A determination to take revenge promptly began to grip his heart.

When David learned of the tragedy that had occurred, he became very angry but weakly did nothing. The Septuagint adds to verse 21 an explanation that David's inaction rose from his love for Amnon, his firstborn. David on various occasions seems to have been partial, weak, and indulgent, failings that could only breed more trouble. But one wonders how much of his lack of cracking down on members of his family rose from the remembrance of his own sin and God's forgiveness for what he had done. Most people find it difficult to punish in others failings that they are painfully aware of in themselves. David's lack of discipline of Amnon contributed to the developing breach between himself and Absalom.

Absalom maintained a total silence toward Amnon and waited for his moment to take revenge. After two full years his opportunity arose. At sheep-shearing time in the spring, it was customary to sponsor gala festivities. Absalom used this opportunity to throw a party at Baal Hazor, probably on the outskirts of Bethel, about ten miles north of Jerusalem. Absalom invited all the king's sons and the king himself; David declined for the reason that he did not want to be a burden to Absalom. It was indeed costly to provide for the king and his retinue at any private or public event. Had David accepted, Absalom could not have taken his revenge under the king's nose. When the king abstained, Absalom asked that Amnon be permitted to come, perhaps as crown prince and royal representative. Whether or not David had any suspicions, they are not recorded here. The permission was granted. Perhaps Amnon himself had his guard down because Absalom had made no threatening moves for two years.

Absalom laid his plans well. When Amnon had been plied with wine at the feast to the point that he was drunk, Absalom's servants were to kill him when given the predetermined signal. Lest the servants fear to carry out orders because of the threat of reprisal, Absalom assured them he would take the responsibility himself: "have not I commanded you?" (13:28). As soon as Amnon had been struck down, all the other sons of the king fled in panic, fearing a general massacre. In fact, the rumor spread quickly that all the royal princes had indeed been murdered. Naturally David and his court were convulsed with grief. But Jonadab, apparently party to some privileged information, assured the king the rumor was false. Only Amnon had been killed for the rape of Tamar. Presently Jonadab's assurances were realized but, of course, mourning for Amnon continued.

There was no place in Israel, (in the cities of refuge or anywhere else (cf. Num. 35:21), where Absalom could find sanctuary. Therefore he fled to the court of his maternal grandfather at Geshur, northeast of the Sea of Galilee, where he remained for three years. The last verse of chapter 13 is very difficult to render. One position accepts the following reading: "He did not go out against Absalom because he was comforted concerning Amnon." That is, time healed his grief and David ceased to be concerned about punishing Absalom. This position is supported by the Septuagint and Vulgate. Alternatively, the passage may be rendered: 'The king's heart [spirit] longed to go out to Absalom, for he was comforted concerning Amnon." With the passsage of time, David lost some of his grief. Absalom was now the eldest remaining son and heir to the throne, and there was concern about the royal succession. The former rendering seems preferable because if the king's heart really longed for Absalom, he would have warmed up to him when he permitted him to return to Jerusalem.

B. Absalom's Return to Jerusalem (14:1–33)

It seems that the first verse of this chapter has been commonly mistranslated and therefore misunderstood. Literally, the Hebrew says, "And Joab the son of Zeruiah perceived that the heart of the king upon Absalom." The second verb must be supplied and the last preposition may mean "upon" in the sense of "toward" or "against." Influenced by the Syriac and Latin Vulgate, translators have tended to choose the former, but the latter seems correct. If the king's heart was longing for Absalom, as the NIV translates, then why did Joab have to resort to a stratagem to persuade the king to invite Absalom to return? And if he were so well disposed toward his son, why did he refuse to see him for two full years after he returned to Jerusalem? After all, Jerusalem was a small city of slightly less than eleven acres; and one would have to make an effort to avoid someone there for two years.

Joab apparently thought Absalom was likely to succeed to the throne and therefore ought to be closely associated with the government of the kingdom. And perhaps he thought that by ingratiating himself with Absalom he might lift the threat of judgment hanging over his own head for killing Abner (2 Sam. 3:26–27). So he secured the services of an intelligent and polished woman from Tekoa to carry his case to the king. Tekoa was about six miles south of Bethlehem, and Joab may have known of this woman for many years. In coming from Tekoa, she lived far enough from the capital not to be recognized and for her story not to be checked on. She did not need to be particularly "wise" (14:2) because Joab put in her mouth the words she should speak to the king.

She was to tell a story close enough to the king's situation to provide a parallel, but different enough to avoid immediate detection of the stratagem. The fact that she had access to the king demonstrated that the common people could appeal to him for adjudication of special cases. In essence the woman's story was that she had two sons who fought in a field, and the one killed the other (shades of the Cain-Abel narrative). Thus she had lost one son, and the whole family had risen up to demand the other son so they could carry out the avenging of blood on him. If she gave up the son, she would be without an heir and the family would become extinct. Conflicting issues were involved: capital punishment for murder and preservation of the line. An appeal to a higher authority seemed necessary to resolve the dilemma.

The king responded with a promise that she considered inadequate (14:8); David presumably was unwilling to defend her son because he would become involved in his guilt. So then the woman offered to take the guilt on herself and won from David the right to bring those seeking vengeance into David's presence for his direct interposition of protection (14:10). She finally persuaded the king to promise his protection on oath (14:11).

After the woman of Tekoa had won a complete commitment from David, she proceeded to make the application to the treatment of Absalom. David was devising things against the people of God in refusing to bring back the banished one because there was danger of cutting off the heir. "When the king speaks this word" (14:13) refers to the judgment rendered to the woman of Tekoa. The king would grant the petition of this humble woman but left his son, important to the entire kingdom, in banishment. She observed that all must die and when death occurs life is irretrievably gone like water spilled on the ground. But God "devises ways so that a banished person may not remain estranged from him" (14:14 NIV). Then the woman returned to her own affairs to lead the king to believe that she had really come for the solution to her own problem (14:15–17). But the king perceived what she really meant, and he elicited from her an admission that Joab had been behind her coming and had put all these words into her mouth in order to reverse the banishment of Absalom.

The king acceded to the Tekoite's plea and sent for Joab to inform him accordingly. In Joab's statement (14:22) there is a hint that he had made the request at various times before. That may explain why the king so readily suspected that Joab was behind the Tekoite's actions. Joab lost no time in bringing Absalom back to Jerusalem, but David tragically did not forgive his son completely. Absalom was confined to his own house for two years without seeing the king. Thus he had plenty of time to nurse his disaffection for the king, and the gulf between them widened.

Absalom tried twice to get Joab to come to him to discuss Joab's mediation with the king on his behalf, but Joab refused to come. Perhaps Joab was afraid of incurring the king's wrath. One did not pester an ancient Oriental king with repeated requests about anything. Finally, in desperation, Absalom ordered his servants to set one of Joab's fields of grain on fire, knowing that Joab would come to complain. This act brought the desired result. Absalom then asked Joab to intercede with the king for him and to state that if Absalom were now deemed "guilty of anything, let him put me to death (14:32). This time David responded with full forgiveness, but it is ironic that this reconciliation is reported as an introduction to Absalom's rebellion. The damage had been done, but David cannot be blamed for all the estrangement.

As something of a preparation for what is to follow, a few notes on Absalom appear in this passage. Like Saul and David, he had outstanding physical characteristics that helped to inspire the loyalty of followers. It might be said that he had a certain charisma. If he was the most handsome man in all of Israel, certainly that would have contributed to his success as a leader. The mention of his growth of hair related to his handsome features, but it also may have been connected with his virility (cf. Samson, Judg. 16). And it may be noted here in preparation for the account of his death. Two hundred shekels by royal standard would be about five pounds. The report that he had three sons and a daughter raises a question about 2 Samuel 18:18, which quotes Absalom as asserting he had no son to preserve his name. Since his sons are not named, as is customary, they could have all died in infancy. Infant mortality was extremely high in the ancient world.

C. Absalom's Revolt (15:1–12)

Three years of estrangement from the court had given Absalom plenty of time to become embittered and to determine to wrest control of the kingdom for himself. Probably not long after his full restoration to David's favor, he launched a campaign to win the favor of his countrymen. First, he assumed a state befitting the crown prince. He procured a chariot (a magnificent one, according to the Hebrew) with fifty runners to precede it and clear the road for him. Thus he appeared to be claiming full royal status already. Second, he deliberately set out to win the hearts of his countrymen. In the morning he would stand outside the city gate and greet those who came with petitions to the king. After a quick review of their case, he would agree that they had a grievance and would promise justice if he were made king. The gate was the usual place for the king to sit and hear cases in the morning. The absence of the king or his deputy gave Absalom a chance to increase the dissatisfaction of the populace with the existing regime. Moreover, when people came to prostrate themselves before him in the usual Oriental fashion, he would treat them more or less as equals—with a handshake and a kiss. By these means, and a variety of other ways no doubt, Absalom managed to steal the hearts of the people.

After about four years (according to the Septuagint, the Syriac, and Josephus in *Antiquities* 7. 9. 1; forty years in the Hebrew must be a copyist's error) of such insubordinate activity, Absalom asked permission to go to Hebron to offer a sacrifice of thanksgiving for his reestablishment in Jerusalem. David, a pious man who would thoroughly support such activity, gave him his blessing and apparently suspected nothing. Absalom secretly sent emissaries throughout Israel. These messengers were prepared at a given signal to sound the ram's horn to announce his coronation at Hebron as an accomplished fact. Hebron probably was chosen because it was his home city and because it had been the royal city before Jerusalem. Possibly bad feeling still existed there over losing the site of the capital to Jerusalem. Absalom took on this pilgrimage two hundred invited guests, no doubt from the better families of the land. These "went innocently" (15:11 NASB), knowing nothing of the insurrection in which they were involved. They became hostages, for neither they nor their families would have dared oppose Absalom. Evidently plans for the revolt were elaborate, much more than the text indicates. "And so the conspiracy gained strength, and Absalom's following kept on increasing" (15:12 NIV).

But how and why could the insurrection have begun at all, and how did it become so widespread? Verse 12 provides one clue. The influential Ahithophel, David's counselor, evidently was willing to join the revolt because of his anger over the Bathsheba affair. Ahithophel was the grandfather of Bathsheba (2 Sam. 11:3; 23:34) and presumably could not quite forgive the king for his adultery and murder. No doubt many in the capital had lost respect for the king over this affair. Then, from Absalom's conduct at the gate, it would appear that David was preoccupied with war and personal considerations and failed to give sufficient attention to the administration of justice; Absalom seemed to capitalize on that fault. Third, some of Saul's partisans probably were unhappy with David's rule. Fourth, the charismatic attractiveness of Absalom could not fail to win some. Fifth, commentators sometimes cite dissatisfaction with Joab's insolence and crimes.

D. David's Flight (15:13–16:14)

Presently a messenger reported to David that the men of Israel had transferred their allegiance to Absalom. Perhaps the report was greatly exaggerated, as had been the rumor concerning the assassination of the king's sons. But David seems to have panicked and decided to flee Jerusalem. Exactly why he decided to do so is not clear. He possibly wanted to spare the capital a bloody house-to-house fight. He may have feared treachery within his ranks or he may have wanted to get away to organize his forces. The city itself had formidable defenses and was capable of withstanding greater forces than any Absalom could throw against it. But perhaps by this time a large part of the built-up area was outside the citadel and incapable of being defended easily. In contrast to the king, his servants displayed a calm readiness to follow his wishes. The unquestioning willingness of his military retainers to do so gives support to the view that his decision to quit the city was based on good military judgment. That he planned to return is seen in his leaving ten concubines to keep the palace.

The entourage stopped "at the far house" (15:17), on the edge of Jerusalem, significance uncertain, where David reviewed the company that had come with him. Besides his family and household staff, there was his bodyguard of Kerethites and Pelethites and the Gittites, six hundred men who had come with him from Gath. David invited Ittai, who appears to have been the commander of the Gittites, to return to his own people. But Ittai declared his undying loyalty to the king. Jewish tradition makes Ittai a son of Achish, king of Gath. Then, while the populace of Jerusalem wailed, David and his company crossed the Kidron Valley, which lies between Jerusalem and the Mount of Olives, and made their way on the road leading to Jericho and the Jordan Valley.

The two priests Zadok and Abiathar, the Levites, and the ark also joined David's company. But the king thought it best to send them back to Jerusalem, both for their benefit and his. They would be spared the hardships of his wanderings, and he would have loyal spies in Jerusalem to inform him of the movements of the enemy. David displayed great trust in the sovereign workings of God and evidently did not place more confidence in the symbol of God than in His personal presence. To strengthen his position still further, David sent back the loyal Hushai to be a counselor of Absalom and to countermand the advice of Ahithophel. He was to be David's spy in the inner circles of Absalom's government, reporting all significant information to the priests, who would send their sons to keep David informed. And David and his company went off over the slope of the Mount of Olives with heads covered and feet bare (signs of grief), and weeping as they walked.

Just beyond the summit of the Mount of Olives, Ziba, the chief servant of Mephibosheth (son of Jonathan), met David with a rich gift. It consisted of two saddled donkeys on which the king could ride (the company was walking in penitence), two hundred bread cakes (shaped like pancakes), one hundred raisin cakes, a hundred cakes of summer fruits" (dates or figs or pomegranates), and a large goatskin filled with wine (16:1). All this was to help provide sustenance for the king's "young men" (16:2), or soldiers. With this gift Ziba won his way into David's heart in a moment of his weakness, and with a gross misrepresentation he was able to discredit his master completely. His claim that Mephibosheth hoped to take advantage of the present confusion to restore the house of Saul to the throne seemed plausible enough, and David believed it without investigation. Then he did Mephibosheth a grave injustice by bestowing all of Saul's estate (formerly given to Mephibosheth) on Ziba. Ziba evidently concluded that Absalom's rebellion would fail, and he sought to take advantage of the confusion for his own advantage. Fortunately, however, Mephibosheth had a chance to defend himself later and to secure some redress (19:24–30).

As David's company came down off the Mount of Olives and proceeded eastward toward the Jordan River, they came to the town of Bahurim. There a certain Shimei, "of the same clan as Saul" (16:5), came out to curse David. This incident helps to point up the deep resentment still harbored among the tribe of Benjamin over the loss of kingship to David and the tribe of Judah. The explanation is provided in 16:13 of how Shimei could pelt David with stones, even though David was surrounded by a contingent of troops and the palace guard. The king's company walked along the main road in a valley while Shimei hounded them from the slope above.

The words of a curse were thought to have power to inflict injury, and the stones were more an expression of anger or insult than an effort to harm. Shimei called David a murderer and a "scoundrel" (literally "man of Belial," 16:7), or good-for-nothing. What he had in mind in accusing David of shedding the blood of the house of Saul is not clear; perhaps he blamed David for the murder of Ish-Bosheth and Abner. Of course, David was innocent of those crimes, as well as the charge of violent usurpation of the throne. Shimei viewed the rebellion of Absalom as just recompense for all the evils David supposedly had brought on the house of Saul.

The reaction of Abishai, son of Zeruiah, was to deal severely with this heckler. He classified him as a "dead dog" (16:9), a worthless person to be disdained; and he wanted to decapitate him. Such a desire did not rise merely from a sudden impulse of the moment but conformed to the legal code that made cursing the king a capital offense. David's response was "What do I have in common with you, sons of Zeruiah?" (16:10). That is, he did not have anything in common with the attitudes of Abishai and Joab, who evidently joined in urging swift justice. He was willing to accept this treatment as part of God's punishment of him and commented that if his own son had turned against him, there was some reason for a Benjamite to do the same. He was content to leave the result in God's hands and trusted that the just and merciful God would turn back the curse and convert the suffering to blessing.

So the company continued on the road toward their destination, with Shimei persevering in his spiteful action. Throwing dirt in the path of the king probably involved more than ridicule; possibly it signaled a demand for public justice (cf. Acts 22:23). Finally the weary refugees arrived at their agreed resting place near the Jordan, and they refreshed themselves.

E. Absalom in Jerusalem (16:15–17:23)

Meanwhile, Absalom and his forces marched north from Hebron and entered the deserted city of Jerusalem without a fight. Ahithophel came along as chief adviser and perhaps the architect of the revolution. But presently Hushai, David's faithful counselor, also appeared to offer his fealty to Absalom. Though Absalom was suspicious at first, Hushai was able to disarm him completely with his declaration that he would serve the one whom God and the people had chosen king and that he would serve Absalom as loyally as he had his father David.

Then Absalom naturally turned first to Ahithophel for advice on how to conduct himself. Ahithophel counseled him to make a public show of taking over his father's harem. This act indicated Absalom's laying full claim to the rights of the throne. Moreover, it would result in his becoming "odious" (16:21) to his father or in his putting his father to shame. Thus a complete break would occur between father and son; David would not find it possible to be reconciled with his son, and the resolve of

Absalom's men would be strengthened as they realized there was no turning back. Moreover, Ahithophel unwittingly helped to fulfill a detail of Nathan's prediction of judgment on David (cf. 12:11). Chapter 16 closes with a note on the widespread regard for the wisdom of Ahithophel and leads into a discussion of the next bit of advice he would give.

With Jerusalem secured, Absalom was now faced with consolidating his hold on the kingdom. The means seemed fundamentally simple to Ahithophel. Absalom should strike at once before David's camp could mobilize effectively. He should use a sufficient force (twelve thousand) to frighten David's little army and scatter them. Then David alone could be killed and a fratricidal war would be avoided. All could then be rallied to the standard of Absalom.

Though Absalom and his advisers were pleased with the counsel of Ahithophel, Absalom decided to see what Hushai had to say on the subject. Hushai argued a different course of action. Evidently pleading with great eloquence that the bravery and military expertise of David and his men were proverbial, Hushai persuaded Absalom to call for a general mobilization. With a vast force they would fall on David's army as dew lights on and conquers every blade of grass in a field. However ferociously David's men might fight them, it would do no good because they would be hopelessly outnumbered. The prospect of a vast army under his personal leadership and winning a decisive victory appealed to the vanity of Absalom, and he took the advice of Hushai. Hushai had bought time for David, and Providence was in the frustration of Ahithophel's counsel (17:14). Absalom and his advisers assumed that all Israel would rally round his standard, but David had considerable support among the people and would be able to raise an army of his own.

Next Hushai felt it necessary to get word to David about Absalom's strategy. So he informed Zadok and Abiathar at the sanctuary in order that they could send their sons to tell David about the two proposed courses of action and Absalom's decision. Since Hushai could not be sure that Absalom would not yet follow Ahithophel's counsel after some sober reflection, he urged David to make all possible haste to get over into Trans-Jordan.

After the initial effort of the priests to go with David, their sympathies could not be in doubt. And if their sons were to be messengers, they could not remain in the city. They stayed near the spring of En Rogel, southeast of Jerusalem in the Kidron Valley near where it junctions with the Hinnom. Apparently Absalom had spies watching their actions. After the servant woman had gone out to deliver the message, possibly while getting some water, a "young man" (17:18; perhaps a servant) detected their efforts to do something important and reported it. When the messengers saw they were being followed, they dashed into a house of friends in Bahurim and hid in a "well" (17:18; perhaps a dry cistern) in the courtyard of the house. The woman of the house covered the mouth of the well with a cloth and spread some grain (or perhaps fruit) on it to dry. Thus the sons of the priests were protected and managed to deliver their message to David.

Ahithophel was greatly disturbed over the course of events. His problem was not mere chagrin over loss of face at the court. He knew his advice was correct, and now evidently he foresaw Absalom's defeat and his own execution for complicity in the revolution. Therefore he decided that it would be preferable to take his own life. Even if Absalom were victorious, Ahithophel would have to give way to Hushai and to live in disrepute or rejection. Suicide must not have been so frowned on as to exclude Ahithophel from burial in the family tomb.

F. Defeat and Death of Absalom (17:24–18:18)

Preparations for battle proceeded. First, both combatants moved east of the Jordan. David the fugitive found a new base of operations at the strong town of Mahanaim in Gilead, the old capital of Ish-Bosheth. Absalom crossed over into Trans-Jordan in pursuit. How long it took him to collect his forces must be left to conjecture; evidently he decided to call for a general levy of troops and to lead them himself as Hushai had recommended. Next there is an aside concerning Absalom's actions, to be followed by an aside about David's preparation.

The detail about Absalom centers on his choice of commander-in-chief of his forces. He chose Amasa, who apparently was the illegitimate cousin of Joab. He was the son of a certain "Jithra" (17:25) or "Ithra," who in 1 Chronicles 2:17 is described as "Jether" (a contracted form of Jithra) the Ishmaelite. This man "went in to" (17:25), or seduced, Abigail, the sister of Zeruiah, mother of Joab. Later (2 Sam. 20:4–13) Amasa met his death at Joab's hand. Evidently intense family disputes lay behind the political squabbles recorded in the books of Samuel. When Absalom's initial preparations for battle were completed, he camped in Gilead, probably not far from Mahanaim.

The aside about David's preparation has two aspects: provisioning and troop deployment. The statement about provisioning effectively demonstrates that by no means all of the people had fallen away from David. Moreover, it appears that the contributions were voluntary, though these men may have received credit for them against future tax levies. Shobi, the son of Nahash from Rabbah, may have been the brother of the Hanun with whom David had fought (10:1). Or he may have been the son of an Israelite, Nahash, now governor of Rabbah. Presumably the contribution represents Ammonite loyalty to David. Makir from Lo Debar had been a friend of Mephibosheth (9:4). Barzillai appears again in 19:31–37 as a very aged and loyal supporter of the king. Provisions included bedding, food, and containers in which to store or cook food or from which to eat it. The major necessities were met. Clothing probably was not needed for what must have been a brief engagement.

David gave careful attention to troop deployment, "numbering" (cf. 18:1) or "mustering" and reviewing the men who were with him, assigning or confirming their officers in their positions, and dividing the army into three groups. One was under the command of Joab, a second under his brother Abishai, and the third under Ittai of Gath, whose remarkable pledge of loyalty to David and evident military prowess had won him a place of leadership in the army. When David announced that he would lead the forces in battle, he was met with determined and heartfelt resistance. His men rightly recognized that if something happened to him, the entire cause was lost; he was worth ten thousand of them. And if the struggle went down to the wire and the last reserves had to be thrown into battle, he could lead them out from the city.

David listened to their entreaty and stood by the gate as the soldiers marched out to battle, as if to endue them with some special strength for the conflict. And he commanded all the three division leaders in the presence of the entire army to deal gently with Absalom for his sake. Not only was Absalom David's beloved son, but also he was God's instrument for judgment on him.

Inspired by their capable leadership, David's men fell on Absalom's forces in the "forest of Ephraim" (18:6). Though the forests of Ephraim were located in the hill country west of the Jordan, the context requires that this forest be in the highlands south of Mahanaim east of the Jordan. Some have thought that this forest got its name from the slaughter of Ephraimites in Judges 12:4–6. "The people of Israel" (18:7), the heterogeneous mass of men who followed Absalom, broke ranks before the highly disciplined veterans of David and suffered twenty thousand casualties. As Absalom's men fled, the forest "devoured more people than the sword" (18:8). That is, the thick forest, the underbrush, and the rocky terrain impeded their flight; and more of them were killed in the aftermath of the battle than in the battle itself. Evidently many were killed by accident as they fell over precipices.

While he was fleeing, "Absalom happened to run into some of David's followers" (18:9 JB). As he was riding his mule (a mark of royalty), his "head" became wedged between two branches. When he raised his hands to try to dislodge himself, he let go of the bridle and the unrestrained mule kept on going. More than likely he was riding without a saddle and simply slipped off the beast's back and hung suspended in midair. The text does not say he was caught by his hair; the historian Josephus stated that. He probably had a helmet over his hair on this occasion; so his hair would not have caught in the branches.

One of the men in Joab's force promptly reported Absalom's plight to him, thinking that Joab should capture him and so end the conflict. Joab's response was that the soldier should have struck him dead on the spot; and he would have given him a monetary reward and a decoration for distinctive service (a belt), and probably a promotion. The soldier's reply showed both intense loyalty of the troops to David and the shrewdness that had made them so effective over the years. His point was that if he had killed Absalom and David had charged him with the offense, Joab would have done nothing to defend him.

But Joab was in a hurry. He said, in effect, that he did not have time to stand there arguing with the soldier. Then he grabbed three darts and ran off to deal with Absalom. Once he had taken the lead in wounding Absalom, perhaps mortally, his bodyguard had no fear of finishing the deed. Perhaps Joab dared to disobey David because he believed Absalom had to die for David's own good and the peace of Israel. Once Absalom was dead, there was no reason for continuing the carnage. Joab blew the ram's horn and signaled a cease-fire.

Absalom's body was thrown into a pit and a huge pile of stones heaped over it as an ignominious monument. Perhaps each of the men of the army threw a stone on the pile to curse Absalom's memory (cf. Achan, Josh. 7:26; king of Ai, Josh. 8:29). This pillar was quite in contrast to the monument Absalom had erected for himself in the King's Valley near Jerusalem. Though well known in antiquity, Absalom's monument has disappeared. The monument of Absalom to be seen in the Kidron Valley east of Jerusalem today cannot be the same one, for it dates to the Hellenistic or Roman period.

G. David's Mourning for Absalom (18:19–19:8)

Now that the victory over Absalom and his forces had been won, the news had to be transmitted to David. Ahimaaz, son of Zadok the high priest, wanted to have the honor. Joab did not want to send him, knowing that David would take the death of Absalom very hard. Perhaps Joab also wished to spare Ahimaaz the unpleasantness or even animosity of David. Joab decided to send a Cushite, a foreigner in Israel, who might be more detached from the situation and one whom the king would not know. Cush was located south of Egypt toward Ethiopia and its inhabitants were Negroes. But when Ahimaaz was determined to go also, Joab permitted him to do so. The Cushite took the more direct route to Mahanaim over rough terrain; Ahimaaz took the longer but easier route along the edge of the plain of the Jordan and arrived first. Why he also wanted to bring tidings to the king is not clear; possibly he did not feel the Cushite was capable of properly handling the sensitivities of the king.

With great anxiety, David was sitting in the area between the inner and outer gates of Mahanaim, where he would be safe and could intercept anyone with news of the battle. At length the watchman above the gate spotted a messenger running toward the city. David concluded that one man running by himself brought good news, probably because several running helter-skelter would indicate a rout. When a second runner appeared on the horizon, David also persuaded himself that he must be bringing good news. And when the first runner appeared to be Ahimaaz, his expectation of good was reinforced because Ahimaaz was a good man. At length Ahimaaz arrived with news of victory in battle but gave an evasive answer to the question about the safety of Absalom. Knowing that a second runner was on the way, David told Ahimaaz to stand aside for the moment. The Cushite likewise brought tidings of victory, but when asked about Absalom gave an unequivocal but discreet indication of his death.

Deeply shaken, David went up to the room over the gate to be alone and to mourn. He paced the floor and wept; the repetitive wording suggests the formal language of lament. David's indulgent paternal affection for his son, and possibly his upset state over the failure of his generals to protect the young man's life, blinded him to the extent of Absalom's crime and the divine justice meted out in his destruction. David did not ask how many of his good men had given their lives to win the victory. Nor did he inquire as to how much bloodletting had occurred in Absalom's camp to restore the kingship to him.

The effect on the army of David's mourning was disastrous, and Joab was informed of the great morale problem among the troops. Instead of being welcomed with a victory celebration, they slunk silently into the city as if they had committed some crime or had fled in the heat of battle. As the situation developed, David took the personal view, that of a broken-hearted father. Joab looked at events from the standpoint of their meaning to the people of Israel, with no appreciation of the grief of a father for his son. Thus the hard-headed warrior spoke courageously but brusquely and almost brutally to his king. His tone and manner reflected an insensitivity and almost an impudence as he administered the necessary remonstrance to his sovereign. Joab's conduct leads to the exhortation that when in the line of duty it is necessary to take a firm or resolute stand, we should do so with all the grace and respect for the sensitivities of others we can muster.

Joab asserted that the king had turned the victory upside down; it seemed as if he would rather have rebellious Absalom alive and his loyal subjects dead. Then he warned of worse consequences, of worse rebellion, if he did not go out and encourage and appease his men. Some read an ominous threat in Joab's words—that he himself might take some action. David responded and sat in the gateway to receive and congratulate his loyal supporters.

Perhaps it would be useful to pause at this point to ask why a person who possessed the many good qualities that Absalom did should go so far astray. Of course, final answers can never be given to such a question, and sons and daughters of the best of homes do lose their moorings; but some contributing factors are evident. First, Absalom was the product of a mixed marriage; his mother was a pagan woman, Maacah of Geshur (2 Sam. 3:3). Second, his father was preoccupied with the responsibilities of state and his extensive warfare; there is no indication in Scripture he had any time for Absalom. Third, he grew up in the unsatisfactory environment of the harem, with its quarrels and sometimes cutthroat competition between maternal groupings. Fourth, there is no hint that Absalom had any personal relationship with God. Fifth, the incomplete forgiveness of his father, which forced him to live in Jerusalem for two years without seeing the king, did irreparable harm.

H. David's Restoration to Power (19:9–29:26)

From verse 9 it is clear that the kingdom was fractured by party strife after the death of Absalom, and David wisely waited to return to Jerusalem until a groundswell of support for him rose naturally or could be orchestrated. Apparently sentiment for his return soon became widespread among the northern tribes, and probably more so among the populace than their leaders (19:10). When support for him seemed to lag in Judah, David sent the priests to take a lead in the reconciliation movement. There is no clue as to what special incentives David may have offered Judah to win back their loyalty, but the hint of the move of the capital northward in the event of their failure to support him has been suggested as a factor.

One ploy he did make, however, was to offer leadership of the armed forces to Amasa and thus to win over the rebel army, which Amasa had commanded. Amasa then enjoyed amazing success in winning the hearts of the men of Judah to David (19:14). Though the text does not say so, it may be guessed that David had wearied of Joab's insolent ways. Perhaps David wished to punish him for the death of Absalom. And David may have wished to extricate himself from the high degree of domination Joab exercised over him. It is not clear, however, how David hoped to dispose of the ambitious and forceful Joab or how he intended to placate the army that was so loyal to Joab. As a matter of fact, Joab had no intention of being upstaged in this way and simply murdered Amasa (20:10).

Effectively persuaded by Amasa and the priests, the people of Judah invited David to return to Jerusalem. A large delegation went down to Gilgal, near Jericho, to meet the king and escort him across the Jordan. Accompanying this multitude of Judeans were two figures who had appeared earlier in the Absalom narrative: Shimei and Ziba. Both had much to gain by ingratiating themselves with the king at this crucial moment. Shimei, who had cursed David so shamefully as he left Jerusalem (16:5–13), now came to offer his loyalty and to win forgiveness. The bringing of a thousand Benjamites represents the acknowledgment of

David's kingship by Saul's own tribe. This adherence was destined to continue with the split of the kingdom after Solomon's death (cf. 1 Kings 11:29–39). David was hardly in a position to reject Shimei and this fealty; so he pardoned the penitent. Apparently David did not revoke this pardon when he made his charge to Solomon (1 Kings 2:8–9) but warned Solomon that Shimei was a dangerous character to be closely watched. Solomon acted accordingly. In granting the pardon, David was deliberately asserting the power that was now returning to him: "today I am king over Israel" (19:22 NIV).

Ziba also sought to win over the king by obsequious activity on his behalf. He and his sons and servants "kept crossing the river to bring over the king's household" (19:18) and to do whatever service might please the king. The reason for this scurrying about was the fear that David would discover his treachery and punish him for it (cf. 16:1–4). When Mephibosheth presently appeared in a somewhat disheveled condition as evidence of the depth of his grief over David's sufferings and his own inability to accompany the king, David already had been won over by the stratagem of Ziba. Mephibosheth got only half a hearing from the king, who did not bother to investigate what had really happened. The hapless Mephibosheth was condemned to share his estates in partnership with the scoundrel who had bilked him of his reputation and goods. David did not come off too well in his handling of this case.

A much happier arrangement concerned the aged Barzillai. The octagenarian had generously cared for the needs of the king while he was exiled at Mahanaim and now accompanied David across the Jordan on the way to Jerusalem. David wished to reward him for his kindness by inviting him to stay at the court at his expense. But Barzillai, poignantly aware of old age, preferred to return home. Those who have had any experience with geriatrics know what a traumatic experience it is for elderly people to be torn up from familiar surroundings. And people of the ancient East had an especial affinity for their ancestral homes and the desire to be buried there. Moreover, Barzillai made the point that he could not expect any special enjoyment from life at the court. Verse 35 does not mean that he could no longer tell the difference between good and evil but rather that he could not distinguish between what he liked and dislike, i.e., in tastes and smells. And his hearing was getting too faint to enjoy the entertainments at court.

He offered his son Kimham in his place as a loyal supporter of David. The king accepted the offer and later encouraged Solomon to show kindness to the sons of Barzillai (1 Kings 2:7). Kimham (Chimham) seems to have received a pension and some land near Bethlehem, which was still known as "the habitation of Chimham" (Jer. 41:17 KJV) in the days when Nebuchadnezzar was in the process of destroying the kingdom of Judah early in the sixth century B.C.

Unfortunately this narrative was not destined to end on such a happy note. The representatives of Judah and "half the people of Israel" (19:40), perhaps some of the Israelites living east of the Jordan and others from the West Bank, accompanied the king to Gilgal. Then "all the men of Israel" (19:41), representatives of the other tribes, came to the king and asked why "the men of Judah [had] stolen you away" (19:41), i.e., taken you away across the Jordan secretly without contacting the other tribes. The men of Judah responded that the king was from their tribe and that there was no need for the Israelites to be angry about this matter because the men of Judah had enjoyed no special benefits from the blood relationship. The Israelites retorted that they had ten shares in the king because they were ten tribes as opposed to the one tribe of Judah (the Levites did not have a separate portion) and so had more claim on David. Moreover, it was their idea first to bring back the king. But the wrangling continued and the speech of the men of Judah became more violent than the speech of the men of Israel.

In this context of animosity between the tribes there arose another rebellion against David's leadership. "There" (20:1), evidently at Gilgal, Sheba, a Benjamite, raised the standard of revolt. Though he must have been a man of some stature to gain such an immediate following, the willingness of so many to follow almost any rabble-rouser is some gauge of the intensity of feeling at the convocation. As a Benjamite he could capitalize on the residue of affection for Saul's dynasty (though most Benjamites present were dominated by Shimei), and as a non-Judean he could gain support from northern opposition to the dominance of Judah at Gilgal. He sounded the ram's horn as a signal to revolt and called on the Israelites to go to their tents. This may seem to be urging them simply to go home, but the term signified secession or leaving their allegiance and became a proverbial expression or watchword of national insurrection. Verse 2 indicates a division of the people present at Gilgal. Apparently the northerners present went off with Sheba, and the men of Judah stood by David "and followed him from the Jordan to Jerusalem" (NEB).

When David returned to Jerusalem, he took two actions, both of which related to his reassertion of power. The first concerned the concubines left behind when he had fled from Jerusalem. As Absalom's commandeering of the king's harem had signified his seizure of the throne, David's rejection of those unfortunate pawns in the political game indicated a reversal of Absalom's fortunes. Since they were guiltless, they were not divorced but were provided for as "widows" (20:3) of the dead Absalom. They were confined to protect David from further enbarrassment. David's second action was to summon Amasa, whom he had appointed commander of the forces in place of Joab, and instruct him to mobilize the army of Judah within three days in order to put down the rebellion of Sheba. Amasa found that to be an impossible task, however, probably not because of his own incapabilities but because of continued opposition to David or resentment over the change of generals.

When Amasa did not complete his assignment within the allotted time, David became very uneasy. Realizing that speed was essential, he decided to wait no longer and to send the royal guard to deal with Sheba. That was an act of courage or desperation, for it must have left him largely defenseless in Jerusalem. He still tried to avoid putting Joab in his old position as commander, however, assigning the post to his brother Abishai instead. This affront no doubt wounded the pride of the haughty old general, but he bided his time until he could take what was not given to him. He marched out to war at the head of his own corps and under the command of Abishai. Meanwhile, Amasa had collected some forces and had joined David's men at Gibeon, about six miles northwest of Jerusalem. He presumably took charge of all the troops there and Joab saluted him as his superior.

Hypocritical Joab went forth to meet Amasa in a ceremonious manner. As a token of respect and friendship he laid hold of Amasa's beard with his right hand to kiss him, as would have been common under the circumstances. Amasa and those standing around were thrown completely off guard. The Hebrew of 20:8–9 is difficult, and it is impossible to determine exactly the intent of the text. It is clear that Joab had a sword fixed in the belt of his military tunic in a horizontal position and that it fell out on the ground. Such an accident would not have occurred if it had hung perpendicularly as in modern military attire. Joab apparently deliberately arranged for the sword to fall.

What happened next is not clear. Joab may have allowed the sword to lie on the ground to throw Amasa and those standing around off guard. He may then have produced a short sword from under his tunic or from his sleeve. Or, he may have picked up the fallen sword; if so, no one would have thought it strange for him to have a sword in his hand while greeting Amasa. In any case the experienced slayer needed only one stroke to dispatch Amasa. That done, Joab and Abishai pursued Sheba.

Joab now assumed command of the troops. And in spite of his wanton act of murder, all the men followed him—Amasa's levy as well as the palace guard. He must have had an amazing grip on the armed forces of the realm. It is significant that a soldier linked the names of Joab and David as he urged the men to follow Joab. Evidently one could not do without the other, even though by now both were becoming increasingly disenchanted with each other. And the encouragement to follow Joab called for an immediate expression of loyalty on the part of Amasa's men, who might have been tempted to rebel as a result of the murder of their leader. Scripture does not pretend to give a complete account of anything, and this military action against Sheba is no exception. It does not seem likely that Sheba moved immediately to the far northern point of

Israelite territory. Presumably Joab's men chased him there, and skirmishes may have occurred along the way.

At any rate, Sheba finally holed up in Abel Beth Maacah, about four miles west of Dan and a dozen miles northwest of Lake Huleh. There Joab's forces besieged him. In his determination to end the insurrection, Joab had raised a siege ramp up to the level of the walls. From that height he was now pounding the walls with battering rams to make a breach and enter the city. Such ramps were laboriously constructed by large contingents of men carrying baskets of earth under forced labor conditions. Assyrian and Egyptian inscriptions show that the practice of building such ramps was common. Perhaps the most ambitious siege ramp ever constructed in Palestine was that erected by the Romans at Masada in A.D. 72.

As the days wore on and the time inched closer when the wall would be breached and a general carnage would occur, a "wise woman" (20:16) stepped forward to prevent the bloodletting. She was a person who, possibly like Deborah, had risen to be a sort of judge or leader in the town. She demanded an audience with Joab. So in a moment of truce, she stood on the wall while Joab stood on the ramp opposite her; and the two parleyed. The exact meaning of the Hebrew text of 20:18–19 is hard to get at, but the intent seems to be as follows. First, a proverbial saying recognized the wisdom of the inhabitants of Abel. Second, the woman averred that the city was among the most peaceable and loyal in Israel. Third, she accused Joab of trying to destroy a city that was a "mother in Israel" (20:19) a part of the Lord's inheritance, meaning that it ought not to be destroyed or depleted. In Israel the inheritance of a family was protected by law so that the totality of the covenant community would not be diminished. Fourth, implied in the negotiations was the provision of Deuteronomy 20:10 requiring Israel, before launching an attack against a city, to ask the inhabitants if they intended to fight. Having declared the city to be peaceable, the woman inquired why it should now be destroyed.

In formal parley Joab disclaimed the woman's charge and set forth the cause of the siege: a treasonous rebel was within the gates and must be destroyed. As a reasonable and patriotic Israelite, Joab took no delight in destroying the city but wanted only the culprit. The woman promised the head of Sheba as evidence that he had been destroyed. Under the threat of loss of life and property of all in the town, the townspeople probably were not hard to persuade that they should execute Sheba. Terms agreed on almost certainly gave even the rebel troops a chance to escape death or exile, and they would not have been tempted to take a stand against the townspeople in defense of their leader. When Sheba's head was thrown from the wall onto the ramp, Joab kept his side of the bargain and sounded the ram's horn for immediate cessation of hostilities.

The clause "each returning to his home" (20:22 NIV) means that Amasa's levy was demobilized and the palace guard returned to their barracks in Jerusalem. The factual statement, "Joab returned to the king in Jerusalem," is given without commentary. But the action must have signaled difficult moments. The king had fired Joab as commander of the forces and had appointed Amasa in his place; Joab had murdered Amasa and resumed leadership of the forces. What went on between the king and his general after Joab's return can only be guessed. The feisty and ambitious general would not be put down easily. And the king, as he was trying to restore his badly shaken authority, needed an absolutely loyal commander who could inspire the loyalty and military success of the army. So a way was found to patch things up between the king and his general.

In the reestablishment of the government, it is quite appropriate to enumerate the members of David's cabinet once more (20:23–26; cf. 8:16–18). Most names are the same in both lists. Sheva succeeded Seraiah as scribe. Ira the Jairite replaced the sons of the king as a confidential adviser. With a couple of sons now gone and shaken by a filial rebellion, David might be expected to choose a personal adviser. "Adoram" (20:24; Hebrew text) was put in charge of the corvée, or forced labor battalion. He is probably the same person as Adoniram of 1 Kings 4:6 (cf. 1 Kings 12:18). The practice of exacting forced labor on public works as a form of taxation evidently developed late in David's reign and continued throughout that of Solomon's.

For Further Study

1. How do you think David should have treated Absalom (a) after his murder of Amnon? (b) after permitting him to return to Jerusalem?
2. How should David have dealt with Amnon?
3. Try to identify the character traits of Absalom.
4. Construct an imaginary conversation between Joab and David as the two met following the squelching of Sheba's revolt.
5. Do a biographical or character sketch on Amasa.

Chapter 8

Concluding Aspects of David's Reign
(2 Samuel 21:1–24:25)

The concluding chapters of 2 Samuel consist of six appendixes, placed here without regard to chronological considerations. There is no indication where some of them fit in the biography of David.

A. The Famine (21:1–14)

At some point in David's reign after he had discovered Mephibosheth and assigned him a place at his own table, a severe famine plagued the land. It lasted for three years and therefore did not seem to be merely a product of natural causes; so David inquired of God, probably through the high priest, to discover if some national and unexpiated sin were being judged. He received the answer that it had come as a result of a massacre of the Gibeonites perpetrated by Saul.

Though Scripture does not record this sin of Saul, David and his contemporaries were probably fully aware of it. Exactly why Saul had committed this crime is as unknown as the crime itself. Probably in his misguided zeal he had sought to remove alien religious and ethnic influence in Israel (21:2), but the Gibeonites were protected by a covenant with Israel and could not be disposed of at will (cf. Josh. 9:3, 6, 15). And Saul's real desire in exterminating the Gibeonites may have been to confiscate their property so he could divide it among his people (1 Sam. 22:7). In any case his personal crime was also a national crime because other Israelites had acquiesced in it and because a national covenant had been broken.

Probably at God's prompting, David called the remnant of the Gibeonites before him to see what could be done to remove the blood guiltiness that had been incurred. The Gibeonites did not want payment of an indemnity, nor did they require victims from Israel at large. Bloodguilt was to be expiated by the family of the murderer. "Seven men" of Saul's descendants were to be executed in a kind of solemn ritual "unto the LORD" (21:6 KJV). The number seven probably was chosen as a representative or sacred number. The form of execution is not specified, but it involved extended exposure of the bodies—a particularly dishonoring and severe penalty. David spared Mephibosheth because of his covenant with Jonathan but took the two sons of Rizpah, a concubine of Saul, and five sons of Merab, daughter of Saul (21:8; 1 Sam. 18:19). It should be underscored that this execution is not to be confused with a pagan sacrifice to entreat God for rain but was a case of retributive justice.

Rizpah, mother of two of those executed, set up a solitary watch to protect the corpses of those exposed from birds and wild animals. Neither the conditions nor the length of her vigil can be clearly determined. She spread sackcloth, but did she lie or sit on it day and night in the hot sun and other uncomfortable weather? Or did she spread it so as to erect a protecting tent? She began her watch in the beginning of harvest (in April) and continued it until "it rained on them" (21:10 NASB), i.e., the corpses. Does this mean that she stayed there from April until the fall rains began in October, or until a rain shower at some indeterminate time thereafter?

In any case the coming of rain signaled the fulfillment of judgment, and the length of time (however long or short) demonstrated Rizpah's great devotion. Her actions stirred David to arrange for those bodies and the remains of Saul and his sons buried at Jabesh Gilead to be interred with dignity in the family burial place at Zela, which cannot now be certainly identified. This action showed that David bore no grudge against the house of Saul. The narrative concludes with the word that God was well disposed toward the land, not because of the burial, but because of the execution of the seven.

To many, this narrative of judgment has appeared to be very cruel and unjust. To help the modern Western reader understand what was involved, several points need to be made. First, the punishment was an example of national responsibility for keeping covenants. Saul's massacre at Gibeon evidently was more horrible than this execution and represented a flagrant violation of Isreal's covenant made with the Gibeonites in the days of Joshua. Second, judgment for Saul's sin was pronounced on him, his household, and his descendants. This execution was part of the expiation for his wrongs.

Third, it is a principle of judgment that God sometimes visits the iniquity of the fathers on the children to the third and fourth generations (Exod. 20:5). Fourth, *lex talionis*, the law of retaliation or "an eye for an eye and a tooth for a tooth" (cf. Exod. 21:24; Lev. 24:20), is a principle of Semitic justice generally and biblical justice in particular. A life must be given for a life; one guilty of murder should pay with his own life (Num. 35:31), and bloodguilt is passed on to members of the family. Fifth, when capital punishment was not administered for the expiation of murder, the land was said to be polluted (Num. 35:33). In this case the land was evidently polluted by the murderous actions of Saul; and the pollution resulted in a famine that continued until expiation was made by the execution of family members.

B. Exploits of David's Warriors (21:15–22)

In these verses the sacred historian presents a record of great deeds against the Philistines by David and his men during the chronicles of David's reign. One reason why the chronicles appear here may be to provide a backdrop for the psalm of chapter 22 in which David praises God for deliverance from all his enemies. These exploits are carried out especially against four sons of "the giant" (Heb. 'Rapha," which may be a proper name for the father of the race of the giants called Rephaim). Though the Rephaim once were numerous in Palestine, few remained in David's day. The exact time of these military actions is not clear. It seems they must be dated in the latter part of David's reign if as a result of the first of them he would no longer be permitted to lead the troops in battle (21:17). These forays were presumably sparked by gigantic champions who gave some new and temporary hope to the Philistines, even though they had been thoroughly trounced by David's forces earlier. Apparently the grouping of these four accounts occurred because they had in common the slaying of giants associated with Gath (21:22).

When the first of these contests took place is not known; but in the midst of it, at a point when David was almost exhausted, he was confronted by one of these giants, Ishbi-Benob. The power of this man is measured by the fact that the weight of the metal point of his lance was three hundred shekels, or about eight pounds of bronze, half as much as that of Goliath (1 Sam. 17:7). As he sought to kill David, Abishai, son of Zeruiah, came to the rescue and killed Ishbi-Benob. After this close call, David's men made him swear he would not go into battle in person any more. They were fearful lest the "lamp of Israel" (21:17) might be extinguished. This figure showed how the life of the people was bound up with their sovereign. In some sense he mediated God's power and blessing to them on a continuing basis as the continually burning lamp in the shrine symbolized God's presence with them.

A second conflict took place at Gob; 1 Chronicles 20:4 places it at Gezer. It may be concluded that Gob (evidently the *Gubbu* of Egyptian texts was near Gezer, about twenty miles southeast of Tel Aviv. There one of David's mighty men, Sibbecai (1 Chron. 11:29; leader of the eighth division of the army, 1 Chron. 27:11) struck down another of the Rephaim.

Subsequently another contest took place at Gob. In this one "Elhanan the son of Jair killed Lahmi, the brother of Goliath of Gath" (1 Chron. 20:5). Evidently there are a couple of copyist's errors in 2 Samuel 21:19; and the correct reading must be supplied from 1 Chronicles, which has been done. The technical discussion of this textual problem is beyond the